New Words, New Meanings

When pupils move from primary to secondary school and start to study subjects in a more specialist way, they have to learn new and unfamiliar disciplinary languages, in each of the numerous subjects in their timetable. These new languages include new ways of presenting ideas, and hundreds, even thousands of new words as well as new meanings of words they think they already know.

Based on a major research project, this book explains the nature of the language challenge students face in early secondary school and shows teachers how they can make the language of their subject less daunting and more accessible for all students. Chapters explore the language of the classroom at Key Stage 2 and Key Stage 3 using written and spoken language data from everyday classrooms. Including subject specific word lists and contextual examples for English, maths, science, history and geography, chapters cover:

- How language use is shaped by topic, context, relationships and purpose

- The language features of early secondary school

- Key principles for selecting vocabulary to teach

- Supporting pupils with disciplinary grammar and style

- Ensuring a whole-school approach to language issues

Full of practical tips to make the language of curriculums less daunting and more accessible for all students making the transition from primary to secondary school, this book will be valuable reading for teachers, educational support staff and school leaders working with children in late primary and early secondary school.

Alice Deignan is Professor of Applied Linguistics at the School of Education, University of Leeds. Her research uses specialist computer software to analyse language. She has studied the academic languages of school, comparing years, key stages and disciplines.

Marcus Jones is a secondary English teacher and experienced middle leader. He is also the literacy lead for Huntington Research School, part of the Education Endowment Foundation's Research School Network. He has delivered literacy training and support to primary and secondary schools across the country.

New Words, New Meanings

Supporting the Vocabulary Transition from Primary to Secondary School

Alice Deignan and Marcus Jones

Routledge
Taylor & Francis Group

LONDON AND NEW YORK

Designed cover image: © Getty Images

First edition published 2025
by Routledge
4 Park Square, Milton Park, Abingdon, Oxon, OX14 4RN

and by Routledge
605 Third Avenue, New York, NY 10158

Routledge is an imprint of the Taylor & Francis Group, an informa business

© 2025 Alice Deignan and Marcus Jones

British Library Cataloguing-in-Publication Data
A catalogue record for this book is available from the British Library

ISBN: 978-1-032-64548-3 (hbk)
ISBN: 978-1-032-64546-9 (pbk)
ISBN: 978-1-032-64551-3 (ebk)

DOI: 10.4324/9781032645513

Typeset in Melior
by codeMantra

Access the Support Material: http://www.routledge.com/9781032645469

Contents

Acknowledgements

From the project

To all the schools who contributed to data collection, thank you for your time, resources and generosity: Beaconhill Community Primary School, Broomfield Primary School, Huntington Primary Academy, Huntington Secondary School, Northallerton School and Sixth Form College, Northburn Primary School, Prince Henry's Grammar School, Rossett School, Stocks Lane Primary School, Westgate Primary School, The Whartons Primary School, Yearsley Grove Primary School.

The project we describe in this book was called 'The linguistic challenges of the transition from primary to secondary school'. It was funded by the Economic and Social Research Council, UK, whose support we gratefully acknowledge, grant number ES R006687/1. Alice was Principal Investigator and Marcus was Project Consultant. The Co-Investigators were Gary Chambers and Michael Inglis from Leeds University, and Vaclav Brezina and Elena Semino from Lancaster University. Duygu Candarli was Research Fellow.

From Alice Deignan

With thanks to Duygu Candarli for her work on the project and her invaluable advice, and to Jane Bradbury for all the chats about teaching and language. In memory of Patrick Hanks, who loved words.

To my sons who I've learnt so much from, thank you.

From Marcus Jones

With thanks to Stella Jones, Lauren Meadows and Andrew Percival for the case studies. With appreciation to Rob Newton, Alex Quigley and Phil Stock for wise words and advice. Thanks to Jane Elsworth, Julie Kettlewell, Beth Mottram and Mari Palmer for ideas and second opinions.

To my parents and brother for being splendid.

And with lots of love to my three best pals: Jess, Clara and Evan.

Introduction

Alice Deignan and Marcus Jones

New words

Words are wonderful things. These seemingly random lines seen on a page hold a wealth of knowledge and meaning; the succession of sounds heard by the ear can unlock new information and understanding.

Words are the currency of classrooms. Teachers and pupils use them either verbally or in their reading and writing, in every lesson of every day. They therefore become a powerful tool for teaching and learning.

That is of course, if you understand them. Or are motivated to understand them. Otherwise, words can become problematic: closed doors that feel off putting and foreboding. To get a sense of how that might feel, here are some words that you might or might not know:

Auricular etiology hypertrophy lumbar nephritis

These are from a computer-generated list of words that are much more common in medical texts than in everyday language. We'd expect that medical professionals would know them, but as a linguist and a teacher, we can say that while a couple look familiar (*lumbar*?), that's as far as it goes.

How about if we try and work some of those trickier ones out from context:

Seizure disorder and psychotic mood disorder are possible *etiologies*.
The patient presented no clinical evidence of *nephritis*.

We could understand the other words in these sentences, but nonetheless, this did not get us very much further, apart from being able to guess that *nephritis* is some kind of disorder. That's enough if we just want to follow the gist of a discussion, but not enough for an academic understanding.

DOI: 10.4324/9781032645513-1

Now, imagine that we're introduced to these daunting new words and meanings, plus another dozen or so, in just one day. And then the next day there are yet more new words to be learned. That can very much be the experience for pupils in the classroom.

The transition to secondary school

The move from primary to secondary school inevitably brings change. Pupils are in a new physical environment: more buildings, more classrooms, more people. And they're now the youngest and (probably) the smallest; they are among new peers, some of whom may seem a bit scary. Even the bravest and most academically confident student will feel daunted by all this at times.

Research has shown again and again that when people are stressed, they cannot learn effectively.[1] Teachers and schools go to great lengths to support students with the practical and emotional aspects of the transition. This book aims to help with one aspect of the academic challenge: words. If your brain is mainly focused on how to navigate the labyrinthine corridors, it is less likely to be ready to take on board the new words it hears when it finally reaches the correct classroom.

But what words are pupils hearing and seeing most frequently in classrooms? Are there any patterns from different key stages and different subject areas that might offer teachers useful information when planning and delivering their curriculum? And in this way can vocabulary offer another mechanism by which to support pupils as they move from Year 6 to Year 7?

This led us to designing a research project, a collaboration between university linguistic expertise and teachers' professional knowledge and experience, to find out exactly what those words are. This book is based on that project.

We hope that classroom practitioners, phase and subject leaders, as well as senior school leaders, will derive use from the data. We think there are opportunities for the findings to:

- Create a chance to reflect on the nature of the academic transition and how the challenge may manifest itself for pupils in your school's context.

- Open up informed discussion about curriculum content, using words as a framing device for that content. That conversation may take place within one school, or across primary and secondary schools to support the transition.

- Prompt thinking about how we can best teach vocabulary in context and what supporting resources may be required, as well as staff training.

- Develop existing activities at the transition to include more focus on the academic aspects of the transition.

This book discusses the project's findings from different perspectives, which mirror the different roles that readers may have in their schools and trusts.

Chapters 1–3 consider emergent themes from the data between the second half of Key Stage 2 (Years 5 and 6, ages 9–11) and the first two years of Key Stage 3 (Years 7 and 8, ages 11–13). This may help frame for school and phase leaders the nature of the challenge that their pupils are facing, informing support strategies to make this linguistic transition easier. In Chapter 1, we talk about the stages of learning words, how academic language is different from everyday language, and how this is part of the challenge of the transition. In Chapter 2, we put forward our view that there is not one 'English', but many, many different versions of English, depending on context and purpose. None of us knows all of these different sub-languages, or 'registers', and we keep learning them all our lives. This leads to disciplinary literacies, a key to success in academic disciplines. In Chapter 3, we explain what our research has shown us about the central vocabulary of Key Stage 2 and Key Stage 3, and give some lists and examples of the most common words at each key stage. This shows a clear movement from concrete to abstract, and a new emphasis on academic ways of thinking and writing in Key Stage 3.

Chapter 4 looks at ideas of interest from each of English, Maths, Science, History and Geography and contains useful material for subject leaders at both phases. It gives the most frequent words from our data for each subject, comparing key stages, and reflects on what these tell us about the goals of each discipline.

Chapters 5 and 6 consider polysemy (multiple meanings) and collocation (which words appear frequently together). These can inform approaches for vocabulary instruction in the classroom – useful for classroom teachers, as well as those who may be determining phase or school wide vocabulary policies. They show the value of presenting words in context, as opposed to isolated in lists, and the importance of not making assumptions about children's ability to transfer their knowledge of everyday meanings of words to the specialist academic meaning.

In Chapters 7 and 8, we provide practical, workable ideas around the implementation of new vocabulary approaches within schools and trusts. This includes case studies, example resources and tools that can be adapted for use, as appropriate, in your setting.

Ultimately, we are **not** making value judgements about what we find. Students need to learn the language of the disciplines that they study as they move through secondary school, and we would never suggest avoiding or simplifying disciplinary language. Neither are we suggesting that students should be making a start on certain disciplinary language earlier. Primary school is the way it is for very good reasons. Schools and teachers are the specialists here. Our contribution is to describe what the disciplinary language is, and present this in a way that might help teachers to consider where they add emphasis in their vocabulary instruction. We hope that this will be helpful, and can inform support for students at the transition, ensuring that words become, genuinely, vessels of meaning for pupils in the classroom.

DEFINITIONS

In case you are interested in the words we mentioned at the beginning of the chapter, these are some (much simplified) definitions.

auricular: related to the ear or hearing

etiology: the cause or origin of a disease

hypertrophy: enlargement of cells

lumbar: the lower back region of the spine

nephritis: inflammation of the kidneys

We found these words by comparing a corpus of medical web texts against a corpus of general English. This is the same basic technique that we used for the studies in the rest of this book, to explore the language of Key Stage 2 and Key Stage 3 across the different subjects.

Note

1 Pascoe, M., Hetrick, S. & Parker, S. 2020. The impact of stress on students in secondary school and higher education. *International Journal of Adolescence and Youth*, 25/1, pp. 104–112.

A change of focus
From child to disciplinary student

Alice Deignan

Introduction

We can probably all remember our first day at 'big school', the 'transition', and the feelings we had. Sir Kevan Collins, former director of the Education Endowment Foundation, wrote 'My first day at secondary school was one of trepidation and excitement. A new haircut and a hand-me-down uniform I'd definitely grow into by Christmas …'[1]. Across the world, the significance of school transitions is recognised, and research into them has been carried out many countries, including Ireland, Australia, Finland, New Zealand and Canada as well as in the UK. The age at which pupil's transition varies slightly from one national system to another, but, interestingly, the issues tend to be the same, whether the transition is at 11, 12 or 13. This suggests that the issues have their roots in the change in school, rather than being tightly age-related. In a few contexts, such as parts of the USA, pupils transition twice, for example, from primary to middle school, then again to high school. Researchers found that for many of these children both transitions have effects, and unfortunately, some of these are negative.[2]

It is not all bad; Divya Jindal-Snape of Dundee University, a leading researcher into the transition, found that many pupils are excited at the prospect of moving to secondary school, and they go on to have a positive experience.[3] As part of our project, we spoke to some Year 6 pupils in England about their expectations of the transition. All of them had some positive feelings about the move. These are some typical quotations, from children from different primary schools (all names have been changed, throughout this book):

EVA: *I'm excited because we'll learn new stuff, so we don't do cooking in primary school but in secondary school we get to do cooking.*

THOMAS: *… secondary school is closer to being an adult.*

ARIS: *I'm looking forward to the PE because here we just do the same thing over and over and over again and they have better equipment there you do different*

DOI: 10.4324/9781032645513-2

things and it's a bigger area to do it because most of the time we have to do it in the hall which is quite cramped with thirty people in.

They also had worries; many of them said that they felt 'excited but nervous'. Their worries and doubts tended to focus on the number of new people they would meet, and missing old friends:

KHALID: *I'm nervous because I'm not a very social person so it's hard to make friends ... and then there's different teachers so you're not used to it here it's gonna be a lot more challenging.*

JACK: *... you might go in a class and then you might call the teacher the wrong name.*

NINA: *but you're like strangers to everyone like in secondary school and even though there's some people you already know and some of your friends are coming those are fine but ...*

In our experience, the social and practical aspects of the transition have been given a lot of attention. Both primary and secondary school teachers are aware that children need some preparation for this big change in their lives. Many excellent transition programmes have been set up around the country, such as visits and taster days, and additional support for children who seem likely to have particular issues. We have found that what has received less attention is the change in academic delivery, and especially, language. We now discuss briefly what research has found about children's first language development in later childhood and adolescence. We think this matters because it helps us to understand the language that children bring to school, and the language that they bring forms the launchpad for learning the language of school.

Language development: how much language do students have by the transition years?

Regardless of the school subject, academic knowledge is mediated through language, and therefore language skills and knowledge are essential for children to be able to access the curriculum and perform well in assessment. Difficulties with the language of school can present a major barrier to academic success. For many students, this is one of several factors, and it might compound other issues.

Counting words and knowing words

An obvious language concern, and the focus of this book, is vocabulary, so the first question we asked is, do children know the words that they need in order to learn? Certainly, at 11, their vocabulary learning is not complete, and researchers have made various attempts to work out just how much they know at different stages of growing up. There are different ways of counting what a word actually is. This is an important question, because this will affect the numbers we come up with. The research that we discuss here uses the idea of a 'word family' as the basic unit for counting vocabulary size. A word family consists of all the forms of a word, that is, the root word with its different prefixes and endings. The word family for *work* includes *works*, *working*, *worked*, *worker*, *workable* and *overworked*, so we count these as one single word, rather than as seven different words. The word family for *factor* includes *factors*, *factoring* and *factorise*, and so on. Of course, some word families are much smaller than these examples; the word *magnesium*, for example, is a family on its own with no other forms.

Research has shown that when children start secondary school they are likely to know, on average, around 8–9,000 word families,[4] and that they add something like 1,000 per year throughout secondary school. Different studies have all found that children's vocabulary grows at a fairly steady rate up to around age 15, when the curve starts to level off slightly until the early 20s. At that point, it almost, but not completely, flattens. Our vocabulary continues to increase throughout our lives, but at a slower rate. One group of researchers tested two groups of adults who were comparable in terms of background and social class, one group aged 20 and the other aged 60. Testing both groups, they estimated that the mid-attaining section of 60-year-olds knew around 2,300 more word families than the corresponding section of 20-year-olds.[5] This averages out at 57.5 per year, or more than one new word family per week. In summary, learning vocabulary is a never-finished job, but the school years are a time when we do a lot of the work.

Interpreting this kind of research is made more complicated because it is difficult to say what 'knowing' a word means: for example: is 'knowing a word' just recognising it when someone else uses it, or do you have to be able to use it completely appropriately yourself? These are sometimes described as 'passive' and 'active', or 'receptive' and 'productive' knowledge. The study of 20- and 60-year-olds, mentioned above, looked at passive word knowledge and might have come up with a smaller number if they had looked at active knowledge. If your knowledge is active, do you have to be able to spell and pronounce the word correctly? What about words that have different meanings – do you 'know' a word if you only know one of its meanings?

Most of us have a large vocabulary of words that we don't 'know' fully – we might recognise them and understand them in context when we hear or read them, but not be confident to use them in our own speaking or writing. For example, I can cope with most words about economics or health that I hear on the news, but I would not use them myself, because I'm aware that my knowledge of their meaning is fuzzy, not precise, and I would be worried about looking silly if I use them wrongly. Children will often feel the same, maybe even more acutely in class, under peer pressure. Or, taking another example, you might have learnt a word through reading, and not realised the correct pronunciation until much later, as was the case for me with 'hyperbole'. I only realised that the word was pronounced 'hy-**per**-bo-lee', not '**hype**-er-boal', when I went to a specialised training event about language. Perhaps it is a trivial thing, but I would have felt embarrassed if I'd pronounced it incorrectly in front of others.

If someone does not know everything about a word, does it mean that they don't know it? It is likely that there is a progression from first encountering a word, through getting a vague understanding of its meaning, then a more precise understanding, to eventually feeling confident enough to use the word yourself. There are always some words which we never learn to the point of being able to produce actively. This is completely normal, and mostly it's not a problem, but it makes counting the words we know very difficult. It may also be a problem in school. Children may have a general understanding of a word in its context when it is used by the teacher, or in reading material, but that general understanding is very different from being able to produce a word, using its technical meaning accurately, as might be needed for written assessed work. Here's an example from my experience which I mentioned above, of only partly knowing words about economics or health. This is the beginning of an article on the BBC news website from mid-2023.

Two of the world's biggest investment banks have warned their profits are likely to be severely affected by a crisis at a US hedge fund.

Switzerland's second-biggest bank Credit Suisse said it could have a 'highly significant' impact on its next quarterly results.

Japan's Nomura said it could make a $2bn (£1.4bn) loss from a US client.

Both have been hit by problems at hedge fund Archegos, which led to the sale of billions of pounds of shares on Friday.

I feel that I have no problem understanding the gist: two big global banks are not going to make as much money as they had planned, or might lose money, because of something that has gone wrong with a third large institution. I can glance at the story and move on. However, if you asked me to use the term 'hedge fund' accurately in a sentence, or match it to a definition, I would probably be stuck. In fact, I would probably struggle to accurately explain 'shares' or 'quarterly results', though I feel I understand all of these terms well enough to follow the news as much as I want or need to. We can easily draw parallels with school students, who may follow the gist of a presentation but be unable to recall the ideas with the precision needed to do well.

The other problem for estimating how much vocabulary people know at different ages is the wide variation between individual children. The research mentioned earlier, on the number of word families known by 20- and 60-year-olds, estimated a difference of around 8,000 word families between the lowest and highest scoring people, in both groups. Differences are not just in terms of the overall number known but also the specific words that different children know. It is usual to know more words about topics that you are interested in or have direct experience of, so we can assume that different children have different patches of word knowledge. We have probably all known a young child with a huge dinosaur vocabulary, or a teenager with a vast vocabulary of contemporary fashion, music or sport. In the past, a few researchers even argued that men and women have different areas of vocabulary expertise, with women using more precise colour terms for example. Despite these complexities, there's one straightforward conclusion: vocabulary learning is very much still a work in progress at the point of the transition to secondary school, and throughout the school years.

Metaphors and idioms

Single words, with literal meanings, are not the only aspect of vocabulary language that is still in development. Research has shown that people are not able to deal fully with non-literal language until mid to late adolescence, and the skill of interpreting metaphorical and idiomatic language continues to develop until and during adulthood.[6] In our interviews with Year 7 students, we found that they did not have an adult-like grasp of what we might regard as quite basic metaphors, such as the use of *current* to talk about electricity, a problem which we discuss more in Chapter 5. Other research[7] has shown that adolescents have some difficulty with idiomatic expressions that we might think of as fairly straightforward. In one study, 150 young people aged between 10 and 17 were asked to explain 24 idioms, such as *breathe down someone's neck* and *go round in circles*. For six of the idioms, including *read between the lines, take down a peg,* and *vote with one's feet*, less than half of the participants could give acceptable explanations. One ten-year-old explained *vote with one's feet* as meaning 'they travelled barefoot', and another as 'not use your brain'. Only 19% gave an acceptable explanation for this, such as 'showed how they felt by leaving', given by a 17-year-old. As we would expect, the older participants did better, but even some of the 17-year-olds could not explain all the idioms.

Grammar

Studies following school students over the secondary years have shown a steady development in their handling of grammatical complexity, and an increasing ability to organise their ideas coherently in their writing.[8] Researchers have concluded that learning complex grammar, or 'syntax', such as subordination and relative clauses (see box), continues into early adulthood. However, there is a huge amount of variation between different people; one study[9] found that a few adults in their 20s produced only the same level of grammatical complexity as primary school children, and vice versa, a few children produced complex sentences more typical of adults. As with vocabulary, understanding of complex grammar almost certainly comes before being able to produce it. The same research has shown that children need a lot of exposure to these grammar structures in order to learn to produce them, so these findings should definitely not put teachers off using complex grammar, as long as comprehension is checked for key messages.

In sum, while we think of language learning as taking place in the pre-school years, and possibly continuing through Key Stage 1, it actually goes on much later than this; children starting secondary school still have a lot of words, structures and skills to learn.

So far, we have been writing about language as if it was just something that children bring to school, along with their school bag, but in fact it works both ways; children learn some kinds of language by way of their school study. In particular, they learn more 'bookish' language from school; that is, low-frequency words and specialised meanings of words, and complex grammatical structures. However, to learn language successfully from input at school, they need to have the motivation

---

Box 1.1 Subordination and relative clauses

Subordination happens when a sentence has two or more parts that have a relationship such as contrast or cause and effect. They are linked with words such as *because*, *although*, *since*, *unless* and *while*.

Examples of subordination, in italics, from our materials are:

- Argon is considered to be a noble or inert gas and does not form true chemical compounds, *although it does form a hydrate* ... (KS3 Science textbook)

- The planters were extremely frustrated with France *because they were forbidden to trade with any other nation*. (KS3 History reading extract)

Relative clauses are short phrases inserted into the middle of another sentence, giving extra information. They begin with a relative pronoun, such as *who, which, what, when*.

Examples of relative clauses, in italics, from our materials are:

- At some points, for long distances, the river divides into two main streams with inland and lateral channels, all connected by a complicated system of natural canals, cutting the low, flat igapo land, *which are never more than 5 meters (16ft) above the low river*, into many islands. (KS2 Geography, reading extract)

- We've got these special birds as a final point *who can who are able to listen to human conversations and then go all the way back to whoever sent the bird and to uh* ... (KS3 English teacher recording)

They are both examples of embedding, which can make processing sentences slower, because the ideas have to be 'unpacked'. Embedding is more common in writing than speaking, and more common in formal language.

to put the work in to make sense of that input,[10] and they need to start from a strong base. In other words, there is a dynamic relationship between language and schooling. As they progress through the school years, children need increasingly specialised language to access the curriculum, and, through being motivated by their academic subjects, they learn more of this language. It is easy to see that for some pupils, this is a virtuous circle. These students soak up the specialist language they need, find the subject easier to understand as a result, then perform better in it, learn more of its language, and so on. It is also, sadly, easy to see that others get increasingly left behind. If they are unable to understand important details of school subject content, they are likely to under-achieve, and may lose the motivation needed to try to catch up. They are then less likely to learn the more complex language required going forward. This in turn can lead to less understanding and engagement with subject matter, and perhaps a general feeling that they are just not good at the subject, or at school more generally, that they just don't get it.

We believe that what we have described applies all the way through the school journey, but there is an especially significant tipping point in language at the primary-secondary transition. We think that this arises from the change in context and goals of school, which we discuss in the next section.

New school, new context

A change in relationships and focus

It goes without saying that there is a huge change for children between primary and secondary school. For many children it is a move from a stable network of a relatively small number of peers, who they may have known from pre-school days, to a large and shifting population of hundreds of other children and adolescents. This change is taking place at over the years where their friendships become much more significant, taking over from their immediate family and caregivers as the most influential and important relationships for many children. Perceived threats to friendships is a well-known cause of transition stress for some children, as we saw in the interview quotes above.

The other important school relationships are those with teachers. In primary schools of course, children tend to have just one, generalist teacher, who is likely to know them well, and be a parent-like figure. This was reflected in a survey carried out by the Times Educational Supplement[11] in 2016, where 2,500 primary school pupils were asked to name what every child should have done by age 11. Top of the list of 100 experiences was '[accidentally] call a teacher "mum" or "dad"'. A large number of the children interviewed for the survey reported that they had done this in primary school, even in Year 6. In contrast, secondary school students are taught by a number of subject specialists and may see eight or more different teachers over a week. Children report feeling worried about this; Jack, quoted earlier, for example, said that he was worried about calling a teacher the wrong name.

In the following interview extract, Emma summarises her anxiety about the new people she has to interact with, early in her first term at secondary school:

> Emma: I liked primary school much better….. 'cos you got to stay in the same classroom you had the same teacher so you knew what your teacher was like like if you go into another classroom and the other teacher's mean …. but and yeah I just like primary school better it's just it's got more space and everything there's not as many people and we've gone from being the oldest to the youngest now all of them like barge into you and they're so scary.

Many children who we spoke to in Year 7 told us that they liked their new teachers, but throughout the interviews, especially with Year 6 children, there was nervousness about the relationships.

As well as the number of new teachers they encounter, children may perceive the sharpened focus on individual subjects after the transition, which tends to be reflected in teachers' priorities. In a study of what motivates people to join the teaching profession,[12] secondary school teacher's responses often referenced their subject. They said things like '[I am] passionate about my subject', 'I wanted to share my love of French', as well, of course, as mentioning the satisfaction of seeing young people learn and get good exam results. A separate study of primary teachers showed that a key motivation for them is enjoying children's company and wanting to work with them.[13] There are no major contrastive studies, and there will obviously be a lot of overlap between primary and secondary teachers, but this existing research does suggest a slight difference in orientation for some teachers: towards children (primary) vs towards the subject (secondary). Academic achievement in the national exams in specific subjects is a central goal of secondary schooling. Ideally, secondary teachers are subject specialists (though in some subject areas, shortages mean that this is not always the case), in contrast with generalist primary teachers. As we'll explain later in this book, we found that this difference in orientation is reflected in the language used.

Language in different contexts

The language of school is different from the language of home and the playground, and it becomes more different as children move up the school years. There is a significant shift at the transition where children start to study subjects with specialist teachers. The Education Endowment Foundation (EEF) write about the importance of 'disciplinary literacy'.[14] Disciplinary literacies are essential for students to succeed in the various subjects that they study at secondary school. Many primary schools start this work with their students and begin developing work on different registers and genres. Nonetheless, its importance increases greatly with the transition.

The EEF makes it clear that literacy is not 'sole the preserve of English teachers'. Disciplinary literacy has two components: language knowledge, and subject specific skills. We have studied the first of these, language knowledge, in a lot of detail, and in this book we will explain our findings and their implications for KS2 and KS3. We found that with each subject in secondary school comes a new kind of language, particularly vocabulary, that is associated with a specific context, topic and task. We go into this idea more in Chapter 2. The second component of disciplinary literacy is the different skills that are needed for different subjects, such as reading for history, or annotating images for art. We didn't study these skills in detail as part of our project so we don't focus on them specifically in this book, but some of the teaching suggestions in the later chapters are very relevant to skills development.

While each school subject begins to acquire its own register, or specialist language, in KS3, generic academic language, first encountered in KS2, grows quickly in complexity. We'll write about what we found out about this language in Chapters 3 and 4.

Not a level playing field

We believe that problems with understanding the language of school can be a major barrier for academic achievement, and that these problems often lead to children and young people achieving below their academic potential. Almost every child will have succeeded in learning the language that they need in order to cope with life outside school, and to interact with their families and friends. They will be at ease linguistically, and are likely to be fluent and confident in these familiar environments. However, often children find that their linguistic knowledge does not seem to transfer to school, where a seemingly foreign and rather alienating language seems to be used. Home language is not, and should never be thought of or spoken of as inferior to the language of school; every dialect and variety of a language is rich and complex, and has been shaped around the communication needs of the people who use it. The purpose of home language is different though. Academic language has developed to talk and write about detailed, abstract, even hypothetical ideas, processes and categories, as opposed to home language, which expresses things like humour, emotion and the stories of everyday life. The language of school therefore has many words with abstract and intangible meanings, and even the words that children think they already know seem to take on new meanings. We write about the problem of new meanings, and give examples of what we found, in Chapter 5.

We know from experience that academic language difficulties do not affect children equally, because children do not come to school with the same knowledge of academic language.[15] Children from lower socio-economic status (SES) backgrounds tend to feel less at ease in handling academic ways of writing and speaking,[16] because they may have had less exposure to it before and outside school. Of course, this is not the case for every child, but it is a tendency that research has found in different contexts. This means that a group of young people are disadvantaged at school right from the start, and often these are children who are also disadvantaged in other ways.

There is a well-attested dip in academic achievement at the transition, from which many children recover quickly. The dip is not universal, but it is widespread enough to be worrying, because it comes at an age when children are especially vulnerable to peer group influences, and on the edge of the stressful years of puberty. The post-transition drop in attainment has been shown to be more severe and longer lasting for students from lower SES backgrounds, as well as for students with low self-esteem and low previous attainment.[17] The reasons for the dip are complex, and can include students' and their families' expectations of education, their economic and cultural resources, and their language experience. We spoke to many teachers and other education professionals about this as we began our research, and we found a general view that language is part of the issue. One history teacher told us:

> Children are able to think but they can't articulate their thoughts because of the lack of language [...] it is not the concepts they are finding difficult at Key Stage 3, it is the ability to access material given to them.

We searched studies of school transitions and found material from around the world. However, although the social and practical aspects had been studied, there was almost no research into the language of transition. We decided that this needed to be investigated, and we designed a research project to study if there is a difference in language between primary and secondary school, and if so, to look at it in depth. The project was funded by the Economic and Social Research Council[18] and took nearly four years to complete.

Our project

The project 'The linguistic challenge of the transition from primary school to secondary school' was a collaboration between academics at the Universities of Leeds and Lancaster, and a network of primary and secondary schools in Yorkshire and the north east of England. The university researchers, between them, have research expertise in education, including science and humanities teacher training, linguistics and computational linguistics (the word lists and information that we describe later were produced by some advanced computational linguistic software). The school partners included Huntington Research School in York, four other secondary schools, and eight primary schools. The teachers who worked with us included Year 5 and 6 teachers, and secondary subject teachers in Maths, Science, English, History and Geography.

We focused on Years 5–8 (when students are typically between the ages of 9 and 13), and we compared Years 5 and 6 (in our schools, the last two years of primary school) with Years 7 and 8 (in our schools, the first two years of secondary school).

To save space, we refer to these as KS2 (Key Stage 2) and KS3 (Key Stage 3), even though the years do not represent the whole of each key stage. In order to find out what the differences are between the language of school in KS2 and KS3, we used a research method called 'Corpus linguistics'. Academics who research language have known for a long time that if we want to find out how people use language in everyday situations, we need to study a lot of examples of real-life language use. Just thinking about our own experience of language, no matter how expert we are, does not give accurate results. Even though we speak and write many thousands of words and sentences every day, we are not good at describing them in the abstract – our brains don't seem to work like that. For example, as an introduction to corpus linguistics, I've asked groups of undergraduate students what they think the usual meaning of *draw* is in everyday English, and which words they think might be found near it in writing or speaking. Nearly all of them think of the 'art' meaning first, and come up with examples like *draw a picture* or *draw a graph*. In fact, a corpus linguistic study of everyday language shows that the ten words found most often with *draw* (including *draws, drew, drawing*) are the following (in order of statistical significance, and leaving out prepositions and other grammatical words like *up*):

attention, conclusions, breath, distinction, line, curtains, conclusion, closer, close, plans

At first glance, I thought that examples with *line* might show the 'art' meaning, but when looking more closely, I found a small number of 'art' examples, but many more like these:

She decided she would *draw the line* at sleeping on the beach.
We have to *draw a line under* the incident and move on.

These meanings and patterns are very familiar once the computer shows them to us, but we tend not to think of them without texts and a computer analysis in front of us. Taking a few example texts is not an answer either. It's only of limited help to study one or two texts by hand, first because they won't represent the full range of texts that students need to access, and second because we tend to notice what is interesting or unusual about them. Often, the most challenging language is hiding in plain sight, and we have to look closely to see what might be difficult about words and meanings that we take for granted. This is where computer technology, in the form of corpus linguistics, comes in. Computers cannot tell us what will be difficult for students, but they can show us what the main meanings and language patterns are, to help us to decide.

The example of *draw* was taken from a large collection of language, or 'corpus', which was designed to represent everyday British English. It called the British National Corpus (BNC), and consists of 100 million words of texts from many sources: books, newspapers, letters, electronic data and so on, as well as transcriptions of formal and informal speech. The BNC is freely available to search on the internet, so if readers are interested, you can readily do so.[19] 100 million words is far too much for anyone to read and analyse, of course, so we use special corpus software. This can count words, search for them and organise them so that we can study their meanings and patterns, in the way that I did for *draw*. The BNC was compiled in the 1990s, and it is still reliable for common, neutral words. To study newer words and phrases, particularly colloquial ones, we also used a newer corpus of spoken British English, called the British National Corpus 2014 (Spoken).[20] This was compiled between 2014 and 2017, and has 11.5 million words. This corpus is useful for words and phrases that have come into the language in recent years. For instance, the word *blog* is not found in the original BNC, but has many examples in the BNC2014 (Spoken), and *download* is much more common in the BNC2014 (Spoken) than in the original BNC.

Studying language in this way, corpus linguistics, started in the late 20th century and is now very mainstream in research. It has proved very useful in many areas, like developing teaching materials for overseas students who want to study a specialist topic in English, but has not yet been used much in mainstream school settings. To get started, researchers need a corpus of the kind of language that they are interested in, which they can then analyse using corpus software. We used a well-known and very versatile software programme called Sketch Engine[21] for the analyses that we've described in this book. All of the various tools that we used for crunching our corpora are part of the Sketch Engine suite.

For our corpus, this meant the school language of KS2 and KS3. We quickly found that no such corpus existed, meaning that the first part of our project would be to build one. To do this, we needed to decide what to collect, and how, and for this, having our diverse project team was essential: the university partners on the team are experts in using the software to build and analyse the corpus, while the school partners are experts in the context and interpretation of findings. We made the decision to limit the subjects studied to English, Maths, Science, History and Geography. These count towards the English baccalaureate, used as an important accountability measure. The EBacc also includes a foreign language, which we did not include, because use of the target language is encouraged, and it would not be meaningful to include non-English words in the study. After consultation with school partners, we collected the following kinds of text:

Written: powerpoint presentation material; textbooks; worksheets; reading extracts; assessments
Spoken: Audio recordings of teachers talking to their classes.

We collected around 4,000 written texts, totalling over 3 million words. Some of the texts, especially from KS2, are very short, consisting of 100 words or fewer. 73 teachers permitted themselves to be recorded teaching, resulting in 175 recordings, and a little over 1 million words. The written texts were collected electronically, and the audio recordings were made by the teacher themselves, using an audio recorder on a lanyard. No researcher was present for the recordings. The recordings were transcribed by an outside agency, who did not transcribe student contributions or any names. As we were studying the language that students have to interpret, not what they produce, their contributions weren't relevant, but more importantly, we didn't have ethical permission to transcribe and study them. We are extremely grateful to all the teachers involved, for their time and effort in helping us, and their openness. We appreciate that it is not easy to have a researcher study your classes.

We worked with 13 schools, eight primary and five secondary. All of them provided texts and audio recordings for our corpus, and eight facilitated of them interviews with students. Five of the primary schools feed three of the secondary schools that we worked with, and this enabled us to track small groups of students. With informed consent from the children's parent or guardian, we interviewed a group of six children in each of the five feeder primary schools, following them up in secondary school. The children's Year 6 teacher chose the groups, which each had three girls and three boys, of a range of abilities. We spoke to all of the groups three times each, twice when they were in Year 6, and once at the beginning of their Year 7. We spoke to two of the groups a fourth time, midway through Year 7, but the Covid-19 pandemic prevented further interviews. Most of this book is focused on our corpus findings, but we will also quote from the interviews to give a sense of how children experience the language challenge.

Some of what we found was expected, but we were able to add a lot of detail about particular words and expressions in different subjects to what we already knew. Some of our findings seem obvious with hindsight, but we had not predicted them in advance. Others seemed a little surprising. In the rest of this book, we first explain what we found about language, and then discuss how our findings can be used to inform and support teaching, incorporating ideas from a number of the teachers who have worked with us.

Notes

1 Higgins, S., Katsipataki, M. & Coleman, R. 2014. *Reading at the transition: Interim evidence brief, report for the EEF.* Durham University.

2 McGee, C., Ward, R., Gibbons, J. & Harlow, A. 2003. *Transition to secondary school: Report to the ministry of education.* Ministry of Education, New Zealand. Evans, D., Borriello, G. & Field, A. 2018. A review of the academic and psychological impact of the transition to secondary education. *Frontiers in Psychology*, 9, p. 1482.

3 Jindal-Snape, D. & Cantali, D. 2019. A four-stage longitudinal study exploring pupils' experiences, preparation and support systems during primary-secondary transitions. *British Educational Research Journal*, 45/6, pp. 1255–1278.

4 Duff, D. & Brydon, M. 2020. Estimates of individual differences in vocabulary size: How many words are needed to 'close the vocabulary gap'? *Journal of Research in Reading*, 43/4, pp. 454–481.

5 Brysbaert, M., Stevens, M., Mandera, P. & Keuleers, E. 2016. How many words do we know? Practical estimates of vocabulary sie dependent on word definition, the degree of language input and the participant's age. *Frontiers in Psychology*, 7, p. 1116.

6 Nippold, M. 2006. *Language development in school-aged children, adolescents and adults*. Elsevier.
7 Nippold, M. & Rudzinski, M. 1993. Familiarity and transparency in idiom explanation: A developmental study of children and adolescents. *Journal of Speech and Hearing Research*, 36/4, pp. 728–737.
8 Nippold, M. 2000. Language development during the adolescent years: Aspects of pragmatics, syntax and semantics. *Topics in Language Disorders*, 20/2, pp. 15–28.
9 Nippold, M., Hesketh L., Duthie J. & Mansfield, T. 2005. Conversational versus expository discourse: A study of syntactic development in children, adolescents, and adults. *Journal of Speech, Language and Hearing Research*, pp. 1048–1064.
10 Nippold, M. 2004. Research on later language development: International perspectives. In Berman, R. (ed.) *Language development across childhood and adolescence*. Benjamins, pp. 1–8.
11 https://www.sundaypost.com/features/ever-called-teacher-mum-top-10-primary-school-rites-passage-revealed/
12 Perryman, J. & Calvert, G. 2020. What motivates people to teach and why do they leave? Accountability, performativity and teacher retention. *British Journal of Educational Studies*, 68/1, pp. 3–23.
13 Pollard, A., Daly, C., Burn, K., Higgins, S., Kennedy, A., Mulholland, M., Fraser-Pearce, J., Richardson, M., Wyse, D. & Yandell, J. 2023. *Reflective teaching in primary schools*. Bloomsbury.
14 Quigley, A. & Coleman, R. 2019. *Improving literacy skills in secondary schools: Guidance report*. Education Endowment Foundation.
15 Gee, J. P. 2004. *Situated language and learning: A critique of traditional schooling*. Routledge; Schleppegrell, M. 2001. Linguistic features of the language of schooling. *Linguistics and Education*, 12/4, pp. 431–459.
16 Patterson, A. 2020. Sustaining disciplinary literacy in science: A transformative just model for teaching the language of science. *Journal of Adolescent and Adult Literacy*, 64/12, pp. 333–336.
17 West, P., Sweeting, H. & Young, R. 2010. Transition matters: Pupils' experiences of the primary-secondary transition in the West of Scotland and consequences for well-being and attainment. *Research Papers in Education*, 25/1, pp. 21–50.
18 Grant reference ES/R006687/1
19 http://www.natcorp.ox.ac.uk/; https://www.english-corpora.org/bnc/
20 https://cass.lancs.ac.uk/cass-projects/spoken-bnc2014/
21 Kilgarriff, A., Baisa, V., Bušta, J. & Jakubíček, M. 2014. The Sketch Engine: Ten years on. *Lexicography* 1/1, pp. 7–36.

2 Language at secondary school

New registers, new words

Alice Deignan

Different language in different contexts: register

We're all aware that language differs depending on context. Within our own lives as adults, we use different words and phrases, even sometimes a slightly different version of our accent, depending on where we are, who we're with, and what we're doing. Within the study of linguistics, these different versions of language are called **registers**. (You might have come across the similar idea of 'genres'; the meanings of these terms are similar, but we stick to using 'register' in this book.)

Our vocabulary choices are heavily influenced by register. For example, think about when we would use the words *weird*, *quid* and *guy*, as opposed to *unusual*, *pound sterling* and *person*. The first three words popped up when I ran a comparative search of a corpus representing an informal spoken register against an academic writing corpus. According to the comparison, *weird* is more than 250 times more frequent in informal speech than in academic essays. In informal speech, people say things like the following (from the BNC2014 Spoken corpus):

It was a bit of a *weird* day.
It's so *weird* cos their voices are actually playing in my head right now.

It does not take a linguistic analysis to decide that the choice of *weird* in these contexts would be very unlikely (or 'weird') in formal writing.

Linguists Biber and Conrad have studied register choices in corpora of different registers.[1] One of their examples is the set of words they call 'downtoners', which reduce the strength of an adjective. In informal speech, the main one used is *pretty* in 'It did look *pretty* bad'. In academic writing, the top downtoner is *relatively*, followed by *slightly*. *Somewhat*, in 'The mother came away *somewhat* bewildered' is used in the news and in more formal speech, and has a vaguely ironic tone to it.

Examples like this ring true to us, and prompted us to explore the different registers of school, to track down the vocabulary that differs from one register to the next, between school subjects, and between KS2 and KS3. Other aspects of

DOI: 10.4324/9781032645513-3

language, like grammar and discourse (the way ideas are sequenced and organised), even sometimes our accent, are also part of register, but in this book we are especially focusing on vocabulary.

What influences registers

Linguists have identified three ways in which different registers vary from each other.[2] Registers vary according to **tenor**, which describes the relationships we have with the people we are communicating with, and the social setting. For example, we all speak differently when socialising with people we are close to than when we are in a professional encounter, or when we are talking to someone we hardly know, and the same applies to writing. Gerry Mac Ruairc, a researcher at University College Dublin[3] talked with 12-year-old school students and his interviews show that they were very much aware of the difference in language used in different social settings. In focus group interviews, he explored their understanding of how their language use was different in the formal context of school, from their informal relationships outside school.

SHANE: *With yer friends yeh can be saying like 'Do you wanna mess around later?' but like in class you would be saying 'What do you want to do later?' It's like more slang with your friends yeh have to be more posh in the class.*

LIAM: *Sometimes I would use bigger words to try and impress people like the teacher.*

CONNOR: *I always talk the right words instead of like saying slang like words I use proper words.*

Similar comments came up in several other interviews:

COLM: *School words are posh words.*

ELLIE: *They say 'That's wonderful' we say 'That's deadly'.*

When children first start school, they may be unfamiliar with the conventions of talking to someone who you do not have a close relationship with. By the transition, this should be in place. Mac Ruairc's interviews show that these 12-year-olds had a very good understanding of it and are able to critique it intelligently.

The students were from different schools, either predominantly working class or predominantly middle class. What is concerning – but not surprising – is that the working class children sometimes found the formal register of school quite alienating.

RIZZO: *I think they're saying that they're a better class than us…*

SANDY: *...and that we're jus like common and they're all posh. It's like if they're saying like we're not good enough and they're trying to change us in school.*

RIZZO: *We're not good enough that's it. They think they're higher than yeh, especially Miss.*

The second way in which language varies is **mode**, that is, the 'channel' or medium of communication. The main difference is writing vs speaking, then there are sub-categories: if speaking, is it planned or unplanned, face to face or over the phone, and so on. An example would be how we might tell someone how to cook something simple, such as cheese sauce. I might begin 'I prefer to grate the cheese before I get started. I'd use cheddar, about half a pack. you'll need quite a bit of milk for the sauce'. However, if you were actually making it with them, in the kitchen, you would use fewer specific words and more pronouns: words like *it* and *that*; and vague words like *stuff* and *thing*, because the ingredients and cooking utensils are in front of you. So instead of 'put the grated cheese in the milk mixture and stir it with a wooden spoon' you might say 'put it in there with that and stir it in with this'. This is very different again from a written recipe, which follows a recognised format, beginning with quantities of ingredients, and using sentences where the verb is in the imperative (the form used for giving orders), such as 'Grate 200 grams of cheese'. There would also be some semi-technical phrases like *low heat* in 'cook the sauce slowly over a low heat'. Importantly, none of these ways of communicating is better than any of the others; each is right for the context.

Mode matters: even the most formal speaking is not like writing, though it is more like it than very casual conversations are. Rules for writing, like 'use full sentences' should not be applied to interactive speaking, and speaking should not be judged as if it was writing.

Importantly, and maybe most obvious of all, registers also vary according to the **topic** (termed 'field' in register theory), so we often find a lot of specialist vocabulary, or specialised meanings of words. In the last chapter, we described research that found that we continue to learn new words throughout our lives, and new specialist words and phrases accounts for many of these. At a gym class for instance, terms for particular exercises and movements are used, such as *goblet squat* and *Russian twist*, that might be completely meaningless to a newcomer, but the terms would be picked up after a few classes, by a process of trial and error.

Learning new registers: a lifelong project

As we've said, we learn new registers throughout life, for example, when we start a new job, take up a new interest or socialise in a new environment. Disciplinary literacies are one form of register, but registers are everywhere in life, and academic contexts represent just one small kind. Once we study English (or any language) in detail, we can see that it is not really one coherent whole, but made up of numerous different sub-languages, that is, registers, in the way that a forest is made up of individual trees.

To give another non-academic example, a friend described going to a UK football match for the first time as a middle-aged adult, when pressed by his young son to take him. Over the following couple of years, he learned a new register, that of the football supporter. This included words and phrases, such as *an empty net* and *on the bench*, new meanings of words he already knew, such as *pass* and *tackle*, and the words of the Leeds supporters' song, 'Marching on Together'. Language is inextricably linked to its social context, and registers are entwined with actions. In the football example, these include dressing appropriately for the match, catching the supporters' bus, and standing up and sitting down at different points before and during the game. In the gym examples above, the connection between the new vocabulary, new actions and new knowledge is also obvious.

My friend's learning curve could be compared to that of a student starting a new school or phase of schooling, but the student's task is much, much bigger and more complicated than learning how to fit in at a football match without embarrassing your child. The student will learn new ways of behaving, such as lining up outside rooms, and, in particular subjects, dealing with equipment or clothing. They will also learn new language, which will include new meanings of words that they already know, such as *isolation*. There will also be many new academic words, and they will get these wrong occasionally, to their embarrassment (just as in the gym example, I initially misheard *goblet squat* as *goblin squat*). Each school subject has its own ways of behaving, and its own register – or, strictly speaking, its own set of registers, as there will be different registers for writing and speaking, and even for different kinds of writing, such as reports versus essays.

Once we've got used to a particular register, and the behaviours that go with it, they become effortless. They seem obvious, and we can hardly remember not knowing them. However, as a new member of the community, like our Year 7 students, the new words, phrases and expected behaviours can seem daunting. Getting them wrong publicly is something that everybody, but especially shyer people, might be nervous about. If we can feel like this as adults, it is so much more difficult for young people under peer pressure, in a new environment, and perhaps lacking in self-esteem and confidence.

Do we need specialist academic registers?

People often say that academic language is deliberately obscure, and that it would be possible to express ideas in much more accessible language. Some of the 12-year-olds interviewed by Gerry Mac Ruairc (above) thought that their teacher chose particular words out of snobbery. There is an element of truth in this idea. Some dialect or slang language forms are regarded as undesirable at school by some people. As a blanket judgement, we would not agree. It is a matter of context – informal discussion versus a written assessment for example. Learning the registers of school is an accepted, and to most people, an acceptable goal, provided this does not come with the implication that children's home language is inferior. (It is important here to separate grammar and vocabulary from accent; there is no inconsistency in using academic spoken registers with a regional accent. Ideally, nobody should feel that their accent is out of place in any context.)

It is also true that some people deliberately choose an obscure word when their message could be explained much more clearly with a more frequent word. This might be out of snobbery, to belittle others, a desire to impress, insecurity, because the person mistakenly thinks that this is what is expected, or a mixture of these. Training university students to write well sometimes involves teaching them **not** to do this, but instead to express complex ideas as directly as possible. However, this is not the whole picture. As school work becomes more specialised, we can no longer explain the abstract and complex ideas involved using everyday language.

Most researchers agree that academic language has developed in the way that it has because of what we have to do with it. As children go up through the school system, they are increasingly asked to think and talk about ideas and objects that are not part of their everyday, non-school worlds, and it is not possible to do this without specialist language. Sometimes this is because subject knowledge involves distinctions that are not made in everyday language. In one of our interviews with Year 7 students, there was a discussion about the new vocabulary they were learning in Science. They were learning new words for types of animals that they would never have to distinguish in this amount of detail outside school.

ABI: *in science we were doing something and it was classification*

RESEARCHER: *classification mhm*

ABI: *and like arachnids and*

WILL: *species*

ABI: *yeah different species like*

RESEARCHER: *species mhm*

ABI: *like fungi and birds*

WILL: *mammals and reptiles*

ABI: *mammals bird reptile*

WILL: *and fish*

ABI: *amphibians and fish and I found some of them hard to understand*

RESEARCHER: *which ones?*

WILL: *that's the one I'm stuck with, phibian*

RESEARCHER: *phibian?*

WILL: *amphibian*

RESEARCHER: *amphibian*

ABI: *yeah amphibian because it's a frog and there's frogs and like toads but some-times there's they can have newts in them but that doesn't make sense 'cos I thought they were like a reptile*

RESEARCHER: *reptile?*

ABI: *so like I thought a newt was reptile but it isn't it's an amphibian*

Sometimes the distinctions are even more subtle, and involve ways of thinking about reality. James Paul Gee, a researcher in linguistics and literacy, demonstrated this. He analysed conversations between 4th grade school students in the US (aged nine to ten, equivalent to Year 5 in England) in a Science lesson.[4] The children had been asked to think about the question 'What makes things rust?', by doing an ex-periment where they submerged things made of metal, wood and plastic in water. He quoted two children discussing what happened:

JILL: *But if we didn't put the metal things on there, it wouldn't be all rusty.*

PETER: *But if we didn't put the water on there, it wouldn't be all rusty.*

Jill was talking about a plastic plate, which had rust on it from contact with metal objects in the water. Peter was talking about a metal bottle cap, which had rusted. Because they only used the very familiar adjective, *rusty*, and they didn't use the less frequent and more technical verb *to rust*, or the (also less everyday) noun *rust*, what they said did not distinguish between the plastic plate having rust on it (a state) and the metal cap having rusted (a process). Gee uses this as an example of how that conversational language is not adequate to discuss scientific processes and states in detail – because it did not evolve to do this. Nonetheless he says, everyday language forms an important basis for developing the registers of science, and a skilful teacher takes students from everyday language through to science registers. As the EEF write, to succeed in a discipline, ultimately, students need mastery of the disciplinary literacy.[5]

Wanting to teach academic language and specialist registers should never be understood as implying that the language of school is better than the language of home. All registers evolve to serve their purpose, and it is unscientific and illogi-cal to suggest that any register is intrinsically 'better' in some way than any other. At the same time, one register can be better for a particular task. Just as the language of home is not adequate for advanced educational purposes, so the language of school is not equipped for the functions of the talk we have with our friends and family. Doing everyday family things like teasing, expressing affection, having arguments about housework and so on using academic language is difficult or even comical to imagine, but our informal, familiar language is perfectly adapted for them.

Since the mid-1980s, educational linguists such as J.R. Martin, based in Sydney, Australia, have argued that in order to work towards social justice, all children need to be explicitly taught the registers of academic knowledge. Otherwise, Martin claims, 'Bright, middle class children learn by osmosis what has to be learned'. He is not arguing that their home language is better – it might be a different dialect from working class children's – but home language is home language, not academic language. He was suggesting that middle class children are more likely to see academic registers outside the classroom, because their homes may contain more serious reading matter, for example. If their parents work in the professions, they are also less likely to find academic and formal language alien and intimidating. Other children, Martin writes, 'whose homes do not provide them with models of writing, [and the knowledge] to read between the lines and see what is implicitly demanded, do not learn to write effectively'.[6] Alex Quigley makes a similar point when he writes about a student he calls David, who handles the disciplinary vocabularies of his school subjects alongside the very different language of chatting to his friends.[7] Quigley writes that David 'will no doubt flourish in school' (p. 75). David is privileged in that he has access to the language of school; other, equally able children do not have this access. We believe therefore that emphasising academic and specialist language should help to support and empower all children. If we don't do this, we are favouring the students who are already privileged.

Our views on register

There are as many registers as situations

We've tried to emphasise in this chapter that we do not think that register is a two-way distinction between formal and informal. Instead registers are subsets of English (or any language), that have evolved to express what is needed, and that go alongside a particular situation. Just as there are an almost infinite number of situations, there are massive numbers of registers. Normally we learn the ones we need to know fairly easily. We tend not to worry too much about them, and sometimes we find the new words and phrases we learn as part of a new register interesting or quirky, before we become used to them and stop thinking about them.

More formal is not better

To take another example: someone who decides to take up rock climbing will have to learn its register, and cope with being told things like: 'there's a hard move to a nasty sloper', 'the intended beta is going to that hold with the left hand' and 'I kept getting stuck at the mantle'. At first, they will probably not understand *sloper*, *beta* or *mantle*. They will also have to learn the names for the various pieces of kit that could save their lives. All this new language is associated with new objects, actions and physical contexts. The novice climber usually, I think, learns these new words and phrases and how and when they are used from more experienced climbers without overthinking them. In this situation, it seems completely logical that specialist behaviour requires specialist language. We can't muddle along with vague, everyday, and possibly ambiguous terms when hanging off a high rock. The novice probably won't feel that the experienced climber who uses the word *mantle* instead of 'transfer from pushing to pulling' is being pretentious, pulling rank or showing off. It is clearly the most economical way of saying what they mean, and it is precise and completely appropriate for the context.

We chose this example to try to make the point that there are no better or worse registers; it's all about situation and context. If a register is suited to its situation, it is good, if it is not suited, it is not. A formal register can be appropriate in the right situation, but it could be very rude, maybe deliberately so, in a situation where friendly informality is expected. We can think of register like the clothes we choose for how we are planning to spend the day. Formal office wear is appropriate for a job interview (depending on the job of course) but not for a football match. The formal clothes are not 'better' as such – it all depends on situation and context. In the same way with registers, formal is not 'better', and it seems to us a shame that children sometimes talk in terms of 'better words'. 'Better' is better for a particular context, not in an absolute sense.

There is (almost) no such thing as synonymy

Linguists generally agree that there is no such thing as genuine or absolute synonymy.[8] There are pretty much always differences between words. Lynne Murphy explains the 'substitutability test': words are only absolute synonyms if one of them can be substituted for the other in every context, without any change of any aspect of the meaning.[9] She shows how even words that are close in meaning, like *safe* and *secure*, or *funny* and *comical* are not exact synonyms. Isabel Beck and her colleagues,[10] writing about words that it would be useful for students to learn, give the examples of *maintain* and *benevolent*. They write that these words are not synonyms of the more familiar words and phrases, *keep going* (*maintain*) and *kind* (*benevolent*). The new words represent 'more precise or more complex forms of the familiar words. *Maintain* means not only 'keep going' for example, but also 'to continue something in its present condition or at its present level' (pp. 25– 26). '*Benevolent* has the dimension of tolerance as well as kindness'. Murphy writes that words that are close in meaning are sometimes different in formality and regional variations. The desire to avoid painful, personal or awkward topics leads to euphemisms like *pass away* for *die*, and *powder room/ little boys room* for *toilet*, but again, these are not pure synonyms, as we would not use them interchangeably in all situations.

Murphy notes that over the years English has taken words from many different languages. This means that sometimes there has been a choice between say the Latin word and the Germanic, as is the case of *uterus/ womb*. Language is by its nature economical, and doesn't usually tolerate new words if there is already an existing word that means exactly the same thing. Where there is a choice of two words, either one has dropped out of the language, or they have developed slightly different meanings, connotations or registers. In the case of *uterus/ womb*, the Latin word *uterus* is mostly reserved for technical medical registers.

All the same, if there are few or no absolute synonyms, there are a lot of near synonyms, otherwise, as Murphy points out, there would not be thesauruses. Thesauruses are highly useful if used sensibly but a recipe for disaster if not! A sensible use would be to look for alternative terms for an idea, but then to check carefully how the new word is used by finding examples in an online dictionary like Oxford Learner's Dictionaries, the Longman dictionaries or Cambridge dictionaries,[11] all of which give examples from real-life contexts.

An example of what can happen when near synonyms are used without real understanding was given by Susan Jones[12] who quoted writing by a Year 9 student:

Briskly, the amount of alcohol intake for young people is rising.

(p. 13)

Briskly seems to make no sense here, until the possibility dawns that the student has searched for a synonym for *rapidly* (and has also misplaced the adverb, at the front of the sentence). When asked about the choice of the word *briskly* the student writer told the researcher 'it's just a word you don't hear very often so it might stand out a bit more'. The educational and literacy researcher Myra Barrs[13] was very much opposed to the way assessment targets have, as she saw it, put pressure on teachers and children to seek more varied vocabulary, at the expense of real meaning and creativity. In her studies, she found that students tended to have thesauruses available at all times when they were writing, to search for synonyms. This resulted in what she called 'outlandish' choices, like 'I raced buoyantly' and 'an enormous carnaging lion'. She wrote that the children 'did not always know enough about the words offered by the thesaurus to choose wisely. Many times children used inappropriate words (sometimes without knowing the meaning) that came straight from the thesaurus' (p. 21).

The idea that there are words that mean the same as an everyday word but are 'better' is, in our view, incorrect. This is the same misapprehension as the idea that an academic register is 'better' than our everyday ways of speaking. In our view, 'good' language is language that does what we need it to do in the context we are in.

When children move from primary to secondary school, the context changes a good deal, and with it, inevitably, the registers change too. Vocabulary changes as part of the new registers. Although, as we can see from interview data, and know from experience, children are often insightful, we cannot expect them to always know what the changes are. We should also be aware that they may be receiving unspoken messages that non-school ways of writing and speaking are less good, and this needs to be countered.

Conclusion

In this chapter, I have put the case that what we think of as a language is in fact a massive bundle of sub-languages, registers. Registers emerge from three dimensions: the social relationships between people participating (tenor), the channel of communication – writing or speaking (mode) and the topic. Registers go with context and situation, and the 'best' register is the one that works in that context. That is, there are no 'better' or 'worse' choices of words or grammar structures in universal terms.

Academic registers are necessary in order to express the ideas and ways of thinking that go with those disciplines. Everyday language is rich, full of humour and feeling, but it can't capture the precise meanings of academic thinking, because it didn't evolve to do that. We learn the registers of home life easily and without stress, but academic registers don't come so easily to all children. They can sound intimidating, and unfortunately are sometimes associated with middle and upper class ways of speaking in a way that can alienate people from other backgrounds. Sometimes old-fashioned snobbery and mockery of non-standard language adds to this unpleasant mix.

We think all children need access to academic registers to support their learning, and in an ideal world, this should be without any notion that one register is 'better' than another – just more fit for a particular purpose. Finally, we argued that good writing cannot be produced by 'translating' words into 'better' ones, because each word has a unique, subtle meaning and context.

Notes

1 Biber, D. & Conrad, S. 2005. Register variation: A corpus approach. In Schiffrin, D., Tannen, D. & Hamilton, H. (eds.) *The handbook of discourse analysis*. Blackwell, pp. 175–196.
2 Halliday, M. A. K. & Hasan, A. S. 1985. *Language, context, and text: Aspects of language in a social-semiotic perspective*. Victoria: Deakin University Press.
3 Mac Ruairc, G. 2011. Where worlds collide: Social class, schools and linguistic discontinuity. *British Journal of Sociology of Education*, 32/4, pp. 541–561.
4 Gee, J. P. 2008. What is academic language? In Rosebery, A. & Warren, B. (eds.). *Teaching science to English language learners: Building on students' strengths*. Arlington: VANSTA Press, pp. 57–70.
5 Education Endowment Foundation. 2019. *Improving literacy in secondary schools: guidance report*.
6 Martin, J. R. 1985. *Factual writing: Exploring and challenging social reality*. Oxford University Press, p. 61.

7 Quigley, A. 2018. *Closing the vocabulary gap*. Routledge.

8 McCarthy, M. 1990 *Vocabulary*. Oxford University Press.

9 Murphy, L. 2010. *Lexical meaning*. Cambridge University Press.

10 Beck, I., McKeown, M. & Kucan, L. 2002. *Bringing words to life: Robust vocabulary instruction*.

11 https://www.oxfordlearnersdictionaries.com/; https://www.ldoceonline.com/; https://dictionary.cambridge.org/

12 Jones, S. 2021. Young writers 'Learning to mean': From classroom discourse to personal intentions. *L1-Educational Studies in Language and Literature*, 21, pp.1–23.

13 Barrs, M. 2019. Teaching bad writing. *English in Education*, 53/1, pp. 18–31.

The academic vocabulary of early secondary school

Alice Deignan

Introduction

So far in this book, we have discussed some tricky aspects of academic language, and we have given some examples from our corpus. We have hinted at the difficulties that children might have with these, and we have shared some extracts from the interviews we did with children. We have also made a strong case, we think, that academic language is not 'better', in some universal sense, than the registers that children speak outside school. However, academic language **is** better for expressing academic ideas, because that is what it has evolved to do. Academic language is not good for teasing your friend about the poor performance of their favourite football team, or for expressing affection to your children or pets, but it is just right for explaining the rules of physics or the underlying themes in a piece of poetry. Without academic language, students will struggle with the precision and detail of academic tasks like these.

In the next two chapters, we give much more detail about the words that we found to be more frequent in early secondary school than upper primary, and more frequent than in everyday language. This chapter covers academic vocabulary across the five subject areas that we studied, that is, the general words of Key Stage 3. In the next chapter, we focus in on individual subjects.

General academic vocabulary

Tier 2 words

The idea of a general academic vocabulary is related to the well-known Tier 2 words, developed by Isabel Beck and her colleagues.[1] We have heard several versions of the idea – it seems to be one of those ideas that has been passed around between people and sometimes slightly simplified or distorted along the way, so it is worth going back to it here.

DOI: 10.4324/9781032645513-4

Beck and her colleagues wrote that a mature literate adult's vocabulary can be considered to belong to three tiers (p. 9). Tier 1 consists of words like *play, dog, drink, happy, look* and *swim*. For most children, words like these don't need any conscious attention apart from learning to read and spell them in lower primary school. Typically developing children generally learn Tier 1 words at home, informally and effortlessly, before they learn to read. Beck et al calculated that there are probably about 8,000 word families in this group.

Tier 2 words are described as 'wide-ranging words of high utility for literate language users.... words that are more characteristic of written language (e.g. *emerge*), and not so common in conversation' (p. 20). Other examples they give include *contradict, circumstances, precede, auspicious, fervent* and *retrospect* (p. 9). Beck *et al.* estimate there are around 7,000 Tier 2 word families. Tier 3 words are highly specialised words, which go with specific registers of language. Beck and her colleagues point out that you might never learn most of these unless you had an immediate need to. I gave an example of a Tier 3 word – or rather phrase – in Chapter 1, *hedge fund*. For school students, Tier 3 words are the specialised vocabulary of each discipline. For KS3 Geography for example, these could include *tundra, biome* and *permafrost*.

The three tiers are often represented visually as a pyramid, with the Tier 1 at the bottom, the widest, base layer, for example in Alex Quigley's 'Closing the vocabulary gap',[2] p. 87. This is a very apt visual metaphor, because Tier 1 words underpin later vocabulary development, and Tier 2 in turn often gives us the explanatory vocabulary to help learn Tier 3 words. In other words, each tier is believed to support the learning of the tier above. We show how the pyramid works in Figure 3.1. We have added an arrow pointing upwards to indicate that in most cases, Tier 1 words are learned earlier followed by Tier 2, then Tier 3. Tier 1 words generally have the most concrete meaning.

We learn Tier 3 words on a need-to-know basis, and our individual collections of these words will differ a lot, reflecting our interests and as we get older, what occupations we choose. The pyramid metaphor breaks down a little here, because there are far, far more Tier 3 words than Tier 1 and Tier 2 put together. There are tens and tens of thousands of rarely used words in different specialist registers.

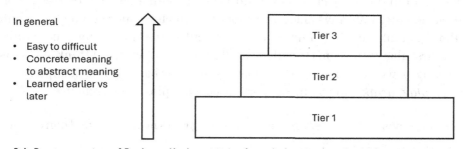

Figure 3.1 Representation of Beck et al.'s three tiers of vocabulary in an individual speaker.

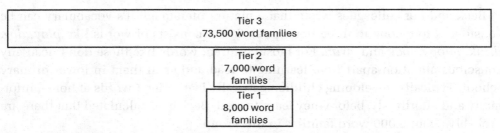

Figure 3.2 Representation of the three tiers of vocabulary in the language as a whole.

Beck and her colleagues found previous research which states that there are that there are around 88,500 word families used in school language. Deducting Tiers 1 and 2, this leaves potentially 73,500 word families in Tier 3. Obviously, any one person would only know a very small proportion of these. The pyramid shown in Figure 3.1 works if you think of it as representing individual speakers' knowledge rather than the language as a whole. If you think of the language as a whole, the pyramid would look more like Figure 3.2

Most literate adults would know all of Tier 1, then a reasonable number of Tier 2 (depending on their level of education), and finally a fairly small proportion of Tier 3. Exactly which Tier 3 words an individual person knows will vary greatly.

We find the idea of tiers of vocabulary a very intuitively attractive idea. It's a really useful way of thinking about different kinds of words, of grouping and exploring them. It definitely has a central truth that resonates with many people. However, a problem arises when words have more than one meaning – an issue which is surprisingly common, and which we'll discuss in more detail in Chapter 5. In an early part of this project, I worked with my colleague Robbie Love to try to find a way of using our computer software to find Tier 2 words.[3] We had the idea that we could run a programme over our corpus and it would spit out a list of Tier 2 words. Needless to say, it wasn't as easy as that.

We used our software to look for words that were more common in academic registers than in everyday language – we thought this should give us Tiers 2 and 3. From this list, we then looked for the words that were spread across different subjects – this should get rid of the Tier 3 words which, being specialised, would just be found in one subject. This should leave us with a neat list of Tier 2 words. What we actually found was messier: a lot of words have more than one meaning, and the different meanings might be in different tiers. Think about the word *energy*. At first glance, it seems that this should be a Tier 2 word – I think… It is used in speaking as well as writing, but it does not seem as basic as the examples of Tier 1 words: *play*, *drink* and so on. Here are three examples of real-life use:

1. She has never got much *energy* in the morning you know. (informal conversation)

2. The cuts could be achieved primarily through improved *energy* efficiency. (from a popular science magazine)

3. The surroundings' thermal *energy* store always increases. (Year 8 Science presentation)

In examples 1 and 2, *energy* seems to be a Tier 2 word. However, in example 3, it is more like Tier 3. *Energy* is a specialised concept in Physics, also used in Chemistry and Biology, and the word means something different and much more precise then the everyday idea of 'something I can top up with a strong cup of coffee', or even 'my domestic gas and electricity'. Another example is *parallel*. This seems like a Tier 2 word when it describes relationships between ideas or moving objects, but it is more like a Tier 3 word in Science, where students learn about series and parallel circuits, and in Maths.

Seeing examples like this has made us think that for some words it can be a mistake to try to put words into one of three boxes, labelled Tier 1, Tier 2 and Tier 3. Instead, tiers are a useful way of thinking about particular meanings and uses of words. The idea is still incredibly important, but we found we are uneasy about imposing hard boundaries between the tiers.

In this chapter, we are not going to try to list all the estimated 7,000 Tier 2 word families. What we will do instead is give a list of the words that are most common across lower secondary school. Some of these words hide in plain sight, and our software has enabled us to surface them and study examples of them in context. We think that it is useful to be aware of what these words are, and to highlight them, with examples, where you judge it could help your students. First though, we discuss some work that was done with university vocabulary.

The Academic Word List

The Academic Word List[4] is useful because it gives a large and very comprehensive set of academic words, used at university level, which makes it a very good reference point for students towards the end of secondary schooling. It was the product of a groundbreaking, rigorous study conducted by Averil Coxhead of the Victoria University of Wellington, New Zealand. Since then, the idea of word lists has taken off and other word lists have been developed over the years, including for spoken academic language.[5] The Academic Word List, or AWL, consists of 570 word families, given as an alphabetical list. To give an idea of the sort of words that are in it, Box 3.1 shows the first ten words beginning with 'd'.

The AWL has attracted a lot of attention. Alex Quigley gives the full list of 570 word families in an appendix to his book on vocabulary,[6] while Beck and her

---

Box 3.1   Sample of the Academic Word List

data debate decade decline deduce define definite demonstrate denote deny colleagues also mention it. It was a very original piece of research which is still very important. The motivation behind the AWL was to help university students whose first language is not English, but this does not make the list any less useful for native speakers of English. In Chapter 2, we put forward the idea that within any language, there are dozens of 'registers', or different sub-languages, which we have to learn as we learn to take part in different activities in life. In some ways learning these is like learning a foreign language.

The AWL was derived from a corpus of texts from higher education from the fields of Arts, Commerce, Law and Science. Within these four major headings are many of the subjects that are studied at university, such as Accounting, Economics, Management, Psychology and Geology. To be included in the AWL, a word family had to not be on a list of very common words, similar to Beck's Tier 1. It also had to be found across all the four major headings of Arts, Commerce, Law and Science, which eliminates Tier 3 words, because they would only be found in one subject. The word family also had to be reasonably frequent – more than 100 occurrences across all of the corpora. We used our corpora to develop a similar (but shorter) list for lower secondary school, and in the next section, we give some of the main academic vocabulary of Key Stage 3.

Finding the academic vocabulary of Key Stage 3

As we explained in Chapter 1, we have corpora of teaching materials from Years 5 to 6, which we call our KS2 corpus, and from Years 7 to 8, which we call our KS3 corpus. This is divided into the five subjects of English, Maths, Science, History and Geography. There is no student language in the corpus, because we wanted to study the language that students face and need to understand, not what they produce themselves. In Chapter 1, we explained the kinds of texts that went into the corpus. Some of the texts that we collected are very short; some powerpoint presentations from KS2 for example, are only a hundred or so words, which made it difficult to create a big corpus. Nonetheless, we accumulated several million words. To try to find the academic vocabulary of KS3, we ran computer programmes that compared KS3 with KS2, and KS3 with everyday language in the British National Corpus (BNC) and the BNC 2014 (Spoken) (explained in Chapter 1). The computer programme we used, 'Key Words', calculates words that are frequent in a particular corpus relevant to another. These words are described as 'key', meaning 'statistically more frequent in this corpus than in the corpus it was compared to'. Key Words are a really helpful way of finding out which words are special to a particular register of the language. Mostly, we compared KS3 with KS2, which showed us which words might be new in school terms after the primary- secondary transition. We also compared it to everyday language, which showed us which words come up in KS3 much more often than in everyday life. We then discounted words that are obviously to do with classroom management, such as *planner*, and words that are repeated a lot because they are in publishers' notes or exam instructions and so on. We have taken out words that we only found in one subject, because some of these will be Tier 3 words. We talk about the vocabulary of particular subjects in the next chapter.

The words and word families that are left, the key words, are the central academic vocabulary of Key Stage 3. Very few words are completely evenly found across all subjects, but all of the words we included in our list were found in at least two of the five subject areas, and almost all across three or more. The full list of 115 words with is given in Appendix 1. We have put them into groups depending on what they are used to do, as we now describe.

The generic academic vocabulary of KS3

Once we had our long list of words, we looked to see if there were groups of words that seem to be used for similar or related meanings, or to be used to do similar things – what a linguist would call 'functions'. We'll describe these groups in turn here.

Words expressing academic processes

Firstly, quite a number of the words in this group are concerned with academic processes, that is, the things that scholars of English or History, or scientists, geographers or mathematicians do as part of their research and thinking. KS3 students are learning these processes alongside accumulating more subject knowledge. In Chapter 2, we discussed how learning new skills in new contexts goes alongside learning new language, and this is exactly what we can see happening here. Table 3.1 shows some of the verbs in this group, with some examples. In the final column for all the tables in this section, we have put the subjects where we found the word. Us not finding a word in our data for a particular subject does not mean that it is never used in that subject. In a perfect world, we would have had access to all the possible data from Years 5 to 8 across the country, but we didn't – our sample is quite big but won't show everything.

As well as these verbs, there are some abstract nouns associated with this group. Table 3.2 gives some examples.

Words expressing academic relationships

Another set of KS3 academic words expresses relationships between concepts, ideas, entities, and, especially in English, individual people or characters, and in History, groups of people and positions held between and towards each other (Table 3.3).

Table 3.1 KS3 verbs expressing academic processes

Word	Example	Source	Subjects
Analyse	... Identifying what you're going to investigate and *analysing* your data and reaching conclusions.	Year 7 Geography teacher talk	all
Annotate	Make sure you have *annotated* your diagram to show how plants adapt to this environment.	Year 8 Geography worksheet	all
Evaluate	Here you can also begin to *evaluate* the causes and think about the most important one.	Year 8 History worksheet	all
	To *evaluate* your science experiments simply answer the following questions ...	Year 7 Science worksheet	
Explore	Who'd like to start off by *exploring* one of the images that I've got on the board?	Year 7 English teacher talk	all
Identify	With a partner, *identify* four ways that you could reduce the amount of carbon dioxide that you add to the atmosphere in your daily life.	Year 8 Science textbook	all
	Write a sentence containing the quotation that you have *identified* as using that method.	Year 7 English presentation	
Outline	...can you please draw a spider diagram outlining the physical properties of a metal?	Year 7 Science teacher talk	all

Table 3.2 Examples of KS3 nouns expressing academic processes

Word	Example	Source	Subjects
Evaluation	And what is the *evaluation* of three times three? Nine, good	Year 7 Maths teacher talk	all
	... A clear *evaluation* of the balance between economic development and conservation.	Year 8 Geography presentation	
Hypothesis	The *hypothesis* that plantation slavery could be reformed and that abolition of the slave trade would automatically bring this about ...	Year 8 History worksheet	Science, Maths, History, Geography
Interpretation	Even the name 'Indian Mutiny' is an *interpretation*. A mutiny is an open rebellion against the proper authorities. In India it is called the First War of Independence.	Year 8 History presentation	History, English, Science

(Continued)

Table 3.2 (Continued)

Word	Example	Source	Subjects
Investigation	What we're going to do is we're going to see which temperature amylase breaks down starch best now we're going to set up one *investigation* in cold water.	Year 8 Science teacher talk	all
Observation	Astronomers are looking for evidence from *observations* of other clouds of gas and dust to see if they can detect planets forming.	Year 7 Science textbook	all
	What *observations* can you make about the poem 'Dust if you must'?	Year 7 English presentation	
Technique	The first experiment uses lead oxide. The second modifies the *technique* slightly and uses copper oxide.	Year 8 Science presentation	English, Maths, History, Science
	Now write an advertisement for your own holiday resort using the *techniques* we have looked at.	Year 7 English presentation	

Table 3.3 Examples of KS3 nouns expressing academic relationships

Word	Example	Source	Subjects
Attitude	We're looking at what the Great Exhibition tells us about people's *attitudes* towards the empire.	Year 8 History teacher talk	English, History
Connection	Can you spot the *connection* between interior and exterior angles?	Year 8 Maths presentation	all
Pattern	In the solid state, a substance's particles are arranged in a *pattern*.	Year 7 Science textbook	all
	Right all of you were really good at spotting this *pattern* we were adding two each time so when we knew what nine triangles needed...	Year 7 Maths teacher talk	
	You start to explore the different sound *patterns* don't you.	Year 7 English teacher talk	
Relationship	He decides to secretly send murderers to kill Banquo meanwhile his *relationship* with his wife is changing.	Year 7 English teacher talk	Maths, Science, English, History

(Continued)

Table 3.3 (Continued)

Word	Example	Source	Subjects
	This type of biological *relationship* between organisms where each organism benefits the other is known as a symbiotic or mutualistic *relationship*.	Year 8 Science textbook	
	A correlation describes the *relationship* between two variables.	Year 7 Maths presentation	
Series	During this year, Napoleon won a *series* of impressive victories against Britain's Austrian and Russian allies.	Year 8 History textbook	all
Variation	These differences that we have between members of the same species is called *variation*.	Year 7 Science presentation	Science, Geography, Maths, English

Table 3.4 KS3 nouns denoting abstract qualities

Word	Example	Source	Subjects
Force	What happens to the speed of the car when the thrust and drag *forces* are unbalanced?	Year 8 Science presentation	all
	The power of Anglo-Saxon kings was limited by the sheer *force* of their earls.	Year 7 History presentation	
Power	To reduce your energy bills you could use fewer appliances or appliances that use less *power*.	Year 8 Science textbook	all
	This challenged the *power* of the aristocracy.	Year 8 History presentation	
Speed	A group set off from home and walk at an average *speed* of 3.6km/ hour.	Year 8 Science presentation	all
	Historian describe the scale and *speed* of changes.	Year 7 History presentation	
Weight	The Curiosity rover on Mars currently has a *weight* of 3,330N.	Year 7 Science worksheet	Science, Maths, English

Words expressing abstract qualities

The third group we identified consists of nouns that are used to refer to abstract qualities. These are mostly dominated by words in Science, but all of these are also found with academic meanings in other subjects (Table 3.4).

Words that have more specific, academic meanings in KS3 than in other registers

The final group that we identified (Table 3.5) is a slightly random collection of words that are 'key' in KS3 we think sometimes because they have a very detailed and specific academic meaning, and a meaning that is stressed in school settings. A few of these might be tricky for students who are used to hearing them with more everyday meanings, which are usually vaguer and more casual. We write more about multiple meanings in Chapter 5.

Table 3.5 Words whose specific academic meanings are very frequent in KS3

Word	Example	Source	Subjects
Accurate	One person is in charge of graphics including a very *accurate* map and possibly a timeline.	Year 8 Geography presentation	all
Constant	Its kinetic energy remains *constant*.	Year 8 Science presentation	Science, Maths, Geography, English
	The rainforest floor is often dark and humid due to *constant* shade from the canopy's leaves.	Year 8 Geography worksheet	
Detect	A receiver *detects* the reflection and uses the time taken to work out the depth of the water.	Year 7 Science textbook	Science, Geography, English, History
Originally	This shows that the site was *originally* a Saxon building and has been adapted.	Year 7 History worksheet	all
Precise	It is easier to be *precise* about younger individuals, thanks to the predictable ways in which teeth develop …	Year 7 History worksheet	all
Surroundings	Some energy is transferred to the *surroundings* due to friction, heating and sound.	Year 8 Science presentation	Science, Geography, English
	… Perhaps indicating to the reader that the narrator feels trapped by his/her *surroundings*.	Year 7 English presentation	
Typical	Identify how settings follow *typical* patterns that allow readers to predict outcomes.	Year 8 English worksheet	all

What do KS3 key words have in common?

Looking at all of these groups, we asked ourselves: what do they have in common? What we saw in all of these examples is a way of looking at the world that is quite abstract and generalised, and at the same time, very precise and exact. In the five different subjects, in different ways, the language we looked at shows a search for general patterns underneath the concrete, obvious detail of everyday life. This is what all higher academic work tries to do, and these words are used to express that. This means that it is not usually possible to find everyday synonyms for the words. It also means that learning the words by themselves probably won't mean much; the words express a way of thinking. If students don't have that way of thinking, the words by themselves won't hang onto anything. Teaching the words in isolation runs the danger of encouraging them to produce word salad rather than do actual academic thinking and expressing it. The words are a way into academic thinking but don't replace it.

Connected to this precision and abstraction, the KS3 key words also lack emotion in comparison to their uses in everyday language. For example, think about these everyday spoken examples of words from our academic list:

isolate

School academic use: 'Describe how to make and *isolate* pure salt' (Year 7 Science presentation)

Everyday spoken use: 'there are huge disadvantages and people feeling *isolated* and stressed out in their jobs'

pressure

School academic use: 'Slate forms when high *pressure* underground squashes the mudstone' (Year 8 Science textbook)

Everyday spoken use: 'you don't wanna have the added emotional *pressure* of feeling responsible ...'

typical

School academic use: 'This persuasive language is *typical* of the genre' (Year 8 English presentation)

Everyday spoken use: 'They're like the *typical* bitchy girls that I wouldn't have hung out with at school'.

connection

School academic use: 'Lots of areas lack energy and *connection* via telephone and the internet'. Year 8 Geography presentation.

Everyday spoken use: 'it's about the spiritual but emotional *connection* you have with that person'.

In everyday, spoken language, all of these words have rather negative connotations apart from the last one, *connection*, which is often positive. (Interestingly, words with negative connotations are in general much more common than positive ones, across everyday English and other languages[7].) The academic uses of these words don't have these connotations. Advanced academic language tries to be as neutral and balanced as possible, not expressing judgements without evidence. This is partly why it is often described as 'dry' and dull. It's is the opposite of informal conversation, which expresses and evokes emotions, often exaggerating feelings and reactions to be more entertaining for our listeners. This is another example of how each register of language has evolved to fulfil a different function.

Key words in KS2

In this section, for comparison, we will show the words that are key in Key Stage 2 compared to Key Stage 3 and as compared with everyday language. As mentioned in Chapter 1, we consulted various corpora: the BNC, the British National Corpus, and the BNC2014 Spoken, for examples of everyday language. In Chapter 7, we'll give these by subject; the words discussed here are across our whole KS2 dataset. We have divided these into themes.

Firstly, there is a large group of words that owe their frequency to preparation for the Key Stage 2 SATs[8] in English, particularly the papers on grammar, punctuation and spelling. These words dominate the whole dataset and include the list in Box 3.2.

Our KS2 texts were collected across Years 5 and 6 by asking teachers to record all their classes on particular days, and to give us all their written teaching materials. The fact that these English grammar words come up as so statistically frequent shows how much this aspect of the curriculum dominates class time.

When we compare KS2 to everyday language, some Maths words are also frequent. These are shown in Box 3.3.

Box 3.2   'Key' English language words in KS2 compared to KS3

clause conjunction subordinate suffix adverbial comma pronoun preposition exclamation plural semi-colon relative passive verb punctuate

---

Box 3.3   'Key' Maths words in KS2 compared with everyday language

fraction decimal rectangle digit denominator cube multiply perimeter triangle diagram angle subtract calculation numerator cuboid

Interestingly, when we did the KS2/KS3 Key Words comparison, these Maths words didn't come up – they only came up when we compared KS2 with everyday language. That is, while these Maths words are not used much in non-school, everyday language, they **are** frequent in KS3. This suggests continuity in the topics covered, that KS3 Maths is building on what was covered at KS2. Both KS2 Maths and English cover some specialised terms, but English sees rather a sharper change in direction at the transition, at least as far as words go.

Other words that are key in KS2 compared to KS3 to everyday life reflect the topics covered in the eight primary individual schools who contributed files of data, and the very concrete examples that are used across a lot of the curriculum. Here are some examples. Box 3.4 shows words associated with the topics of Egyptians, Vikings, the development of the railway, South America, animals and evolution.

As we explored the KS2 word lists, we kept seeing a tendency for materials and teachers to use very concrete examples to make academic topics real and immediate to students. There are clearly very sound pedagogical reasons for this. There are also very good reasons why KS3 begins to prepare students for the more abstract reasoning that is needed as students move up through the school years. What may throw some students off balance at the primary-secondary transition is what seems to be quite an abrupt change in this orientation.

Box 3.4   'Key' KS2 words that are topic-focused

afterlife ancient bumblebee chocolate Darwin earthquake Edison Egyptian evolution fossil insect locomotive mammal Mayan micro-organism mummy ocean panda pharaoh pizza pollen pyramid railway river seed tributary vertebrate Viking whale wing

---

Box 3.5   A practical question

Thinking about your own subject area or year group, do you think that we are correct in suggesting that there is a rather abrupt move from concrete, everyday examples to abstract reasoning?

If so, and given the move from concrete to abstract has to be made in order for students to succeed further along in their education, is there any way this can be eased or supported?

We do not think that the answer lies in trying to make KS2 more like KS3. Similarly, delaying the abstract reasoning and language that is needed in KS3 might disadvantage students. We think the answer lies in making the move more explicit, and giving language and conceptual support. In Chapters 7 and 8 we offer some suggestions as to how this could be done.

Final thoughts

Some issues with word lists

So, how useful are word list like these, in themselves? Potentially, they could be very useful indeed, as they immediately help us to see where problems might come up. As we have tried to do here, word lists can be gone through to find themes. They can show up trends across year groups and subjects, like the move from concrete to abstract, that are obvious when we look back at them but might not have seen so clearly before. Also, of course, the lists can suggest particular words that might warrant more attention.

What depth of knowledge do students need?

In Chapter 1, we discussed the idea of passive and active vocabulary knowledge, often called receptive and productive[9] knowledge. I wrote about the huge difference between each individual's passive and active vocabulary size; we all understand far more words than we can produce. Beck and her colleagues[10] wrote that there are various stages along the scale from not knowing to knowing a word. They write that we can go from not knowing a word to having a very general idea of it, in their example, knowing that *mendacious* has a negative meaning but not knowing exactly what that is. Then comes a very narrow understanding of a word, perhaps in just a single context. This was seen in EAL learners by one researcher,[11] who found that the Year 5 pupils she observed were only able to define and use words in the same very narrow context that they had learned them in. The next stage is knowing a word but not being able to recall it readily to be able to use it, and finally, we have a full knowledge of a word when we are able to use it accurately and understand how its meaning relates to other words.

Importantly, it may not be a problem at all if we only know a word vaguely or passively rather than completely and actively. We all go through life only half knowing a large proportion of the words we read and hear, and this might never cause us problems. So, looking at a word list, we need to think about whether our students need to know words actively, that is, to be able to produce them accurately, or whether it is enough to have a general idea of meaning and recognise them when they read or hear them. Time and cognitive capacity are finite. These important questions are taken up again later in this book.

Notes

1 Beck, I., McKeown, M. & Kucan, L. 2002. *Bringing words to life: Robust vocabulary instruction.* Guilford Press.
2 Quigley, A. 2018. *Closing the vocabulary gap.* Routledge.

3 Deignan, A. & Love, R. 2021. Using corpus methods to identify subject specific uses of polysemous words in English secondary school science materials. *Corpora*, 16/2, pp. 165–189.

4 Cox, A. 2000. A new academic word list. *TESOL Quarterly*, 34/2, pp. 213–238

5 Dang, T. N. Y., Coxhead, A. & Webb, S. 2017. The academic spoken word list. *Language Learning*, 67/4, pp. 959–997.

6 Quigley, A. 2018. *Closing the vocabulary gap*. Routledge.

7 Moon, R. 1998. Fixed expressions and idioms in English: A corpus-based study. Clarendon; Braasch, A. & Pedersen, B. 2010. *Encoding attitude and connotation in wordnets*. Paper presented to Euralex conference.

8 Standard Assessment Tests; tests administered in Year 2 and in year 6 towards the end of the final year in primary school.

9 Schmitt, N. 2014. Size and depth of vocabulary knowledge: What the research shows. *Language Learning*, 64/4, pp. 9130951.

10 Beck, I., McKeown, M. & Omanson, R. C. 1987. The effects and uses of diverse vocabulary instructional techniques. In McKeown, H. & Curtis, M. (eds.) *The nature of vocabulary acquisition*. Erlbaum, pp. 147– 163.

11 Robinson, P. 2005. Teaching key vocabulary in Geography and Science classrooms: An analysis of teachers' practice with particular reference to EAL pupils' learning. *Language and Education,* 19/5, pp. 428–445.

Vocabulary across subjects

Alice Deignan

Introduction

We begin with an extract from a government report[1]:

> For the initial Track-1 business model, a fixed trajectory reference price was published in advance of contract negotiations as a stable analogue to the carbon market price to provide predictability to investors in respect of support payments and reduce subsidy over time. It has always been our intention to evolve this position to a reference price that is linked to an Emitter's carbon price exposure.

Possibly, like me, you would struggle to make sense of this. Knowing that it comes from a report called 'Carbon capture, usage and storage' may help a little, but for me that still does not get me anywhere near full comprehension. I have a rough idea of most of the words, though would be hard pushed to define *analogue*, among others, and I suspect the use of *exposure* might not be the one I'm familiar with. Some of the words appear in clusters, where I feel I might know the separate words but I don't know what they mean when they fit together, like *fixed trajectory reference price*. My problem is that this is a register, technical government reports, that I have very little experience of. I also don't know much about the topics of the report: carbon capture and business models. I got more out of the extract at second and third readings, but in normal life I might not have time to do this.

In Chapter 2, we put forward the idea that far from being a single language, English (and every other language) is a composite of many different registers. No individual person will know every register of the language, and we learn new registers throughout our lives, for example, if we start a new job or take up a new interest. If it is something like a new sport or creative interest, we might learn the new register without too much difficulty and even enjoy it. Academic registers can be more demanding, because as well as involving rather daunting, hard new words, they can go along with very specialised and conceptually difficult knowledge, and new

DOI: 10.4324/9781032645513-5

ways of thinking and organising ideas. The extract above is an example of a register that is challenging to me because I don't understand some of the language used, nor the background ideas and what the report is setting out to do.

Off-putting as it sometimes is, learning disciplinary registers is a major part of moving up through school successfully. The language of the new register can't be detached from the ways of thinking and behaving that go with it. In this chapter, we will look at the five core subjects separately, and list the words that we found were most frequent in each of them, in KS3 compared to KS2. This will give a set of disciplinary vocabularies. To find the words of these new registers, we compared KS3 with KS2 data for each subject. We've left out words that are used for classroom management or are in the headers or footers of worksheets or presentations in order to focus on the words of the discipline itself.

Maths

Previous studies

Our day-to-day experience suggests that of all school subjects, Maths tends to be the one that both children and adults in the UK are most likely to feel anxious and negative about. This is confirmed by research studies like that of Dowker and colleagues, who found evidence of longstanding maths anxiety.[2] One of the difficulties students face is the language of Maths. Researchers now agree that learning Maths cannot be separated from learning the language of Maths.[3]

Thompson and Rubenstein[4] studied the vocabulary of Maths, in an article that begins with the question 'Do your students speak mathematics, or do they think that the mathematics classroom is another country where they must use a foreign language?' They analysed potential problems with the vocabulary of Maths, beginning with words that have two or more meanings – an everyday meaning and a Maths one. They talk about words having different meanings when used as part of a phrase, and words which actually have different meanings within different branches of Maths. Some of their categories and examples are in Table 4.1.

In order to see if and how this applies for the transition years, we crunched our corpus data for Maths, as described in the chapter introduction, and describe the main themes in the next sections.

Key words

As in Chapter 3, we used the Key Words software, to compare words in KS3 Maths against KS2 Maths. This showed us which words are statistically more frequent in KS3 Maths, then we did the reverse comparison, KS2 against KS3. Tables 4.2 and 4.3 give the top 30 key words for each calculation, presented in alphabetical order.

The key words in KS2 compared to KS3 contain a large number of nouns for everyday objects.

Table 4.1 Potential pitfalls in Maths vocabulary, from Thompson & Rubenstein's 2000 article

Potential pitfall	Example
A Maths word is the same as the everyday one, but has a different meaning	Prime, power, factor, mode, event,
The Maths meaning of a word is similar to everyday one but much more precise	Equivalent, slope, reflection, average
A Maths word is unique to Maths	Decimal, quotient, isosceles, outlier
The meaning of a Maths word may be changed by the word that comes before it	(Square) root, (regular) polygon, (arithmetic) sequence
A word is shared by Maths and Science but has different meanings in each	Solution, variable, degree, element, cell

Table 4.2 Key Words in KS3 compared to KS2

Alternate	Elevation	Increase	Negative	Rotational
Angles	Enlarge (ment)	Indices	pi	Significant
Corresponding	Expand	Interior	Power	Symmetry
Data	Exterior	Median	Random	Sample
Decrease	Factorise	Mode	Probability	Scatter
Discrete	Frequency	Multiplier	Proportional	Substitute

Table 4.3 Key Words in KS2 compared to KS3

Apple	Elf	Leaflet	Parachute	Sack
Apricot	Flower	Measurer	Peanut	Shadow
Banana	Gift	Melon	Pineapple	Strip
Cashew	Halve	Model	Plank	Teddy
Christmas	Identical	Numeral	Roman	Tray
Crayon	Jar	Nut	Santa	Tulip

In the next sections we'll describe what we think are the important points about these tables.

Concrete and abstract

The main theme that comes out of Table 4.3, KS2 words compared to KS3, is the sheer number of words for concrete, everyday objects. This is because problems are expressed in terms of everyday situations, which are chosen because children might be able to relate to them, and to prepare them for the KS2 Maths SAT papers (2 and 3) which use a lot of concrete examples. For example, *jar* is frequent because textbooks and worksheets have a lot of problems involving jars of jam, chocolate and sweets, like this one:

> A jar contains 30 sweets. The weight of the jar and the sweets is 620g. David eats 12 sweets. The weight of the jar and the sweets is now 440g. How much does the jar weigh? Year 6 worksheet.

This does not mean that there are no specialised Maths words in the KS2 Maths corpus. If we compare it against everyday English, using the BNC (as opposed to against KS3 like we did to get Table 4.3), many basic Maths words come up; see Table 4.4.

Because these words are also found in KS3, they didn't show up when KS2 and KS3 Maths were compared. This is an indication of consistency, that the mathematical language introduced in KS2 is recycled and built on in KS3.

Moving on to KS3, the KS3/2 key words show just how much new mathematical language there is after the transition, and how different in nature it is from KS2. Overwhelmingly, it is abstract, with no more apples, jars of jam, shadows and planks. In KS3, problems are mostly framed in pure mathematical terms, with, as well as new specialist words, a large amount of new symbols. For comparison, a task using graphs in our KS2 corpus is:

> The graph shows the temperature recorded in a town one day last summer. How much did the temperature increase by between 9am and 2pm? Year 6 worksheet

A task using graphs in the KS3 corpus is:

> Draw the graph $y = 2x + 3$. Now using your protractor or set square draw a graph that is perpendicular to $y = 2x + 3$. Calculate the gradient of the new graph and write it down. Year 7 presentation.

The second task is not related to any real-world context – though of course, this kind of knowledge can be and is applied all sorts of real-world situations. There are some tasks of this kind in our KS2 data but they are heavily outweighed by the more concrete examples. Obviously, it is normal for tasks to get harder as children

Table 4.4 Top 20 Key Words in KS2 Maths compared with everyday language

Angle	Decimal	Divide	Multiply	Rectangle
Calculation	Denominator	Fraction	Numerator	Subtract
Cube	Diagram	Multiple	Perimeter	Triangle
Cuboid	Digit	Multiplication	Quadrilateral	Vertices

progress through school, and there would be something very wrong if they did not. What we saw in the KS2/3 comparison though was quite a sudden difference in the nature of the language. Underneath the concrete examples or algebra, the step up in the actual mathematical level might not always be too challenging, but the switch from concrete examples to abstract reasoning may be a tough one for some children.

Multiple meanings

In the top 30 KS3 Maths Key Words, we found nine that have a different meaning in Maths from everyday language, shown in Box 4.1.

Box 4.1   KS3 Maths Key Words with more than one meaning

alternate corresponding expand exterior interior mode power scatter substitute

---

In Appendix 2 we give corpus examples of each meaning that we found, and in the next chapter we explore the problem of multiple meanings across registers.

The grammar of Maths language

Our focus in this book is vocabulary, but it is important to note here as well a shift in the grammar between KS2 and KS3 in Maths. Analysis by the project researchers, Duygu Candarli and Florence Oxley, found that Maths sentences in KS2 tend to be quite a lot like sentences in everyday conversational language.[5] The KS2 sentences use present tense verbs, verbs that report speech, like *say* and *tell*, and people's names. These sentences are from our KS2 Maths corpus:

> To find percentages of quantities, Lucy says '10% = 1/10 so to find 10% of a number you divide it by 10'. Ross says 'So to find 25% of a number you divide it by 25'. What do you think? Year 6 Maths presentation.

These sentences are grammatically similar to everyday spoken language, in that they contain present tense verbs and names, report speech directly, and are interactive, asking for the reader's opinion.

In contrast, KS3 Maths sentences use '-ing' verb forms as if they were nouns, and other noun forms that compress abstract concepts. For example, this is from KS3:

> If an event E is impossible, the probability of its happening is 0. Year 8 Maths worksheet.

Here, we have the abstract noun *probability*, and the '-ing' form *happening*, which turns the verb *happen* into an abstract noun, a 'thing'. Linguists call this act of turning verbs, which describe actions or processes, into nouns 'nominalisation', as we describe in Box 4.2.

Box 4.2   Nominalisation

Nominalisation means turning a verb (or sometimes, an adjective) into a noun.

The most obvious, default way of describing an action is by using a verb, and this is what we usually do in informal speech. Look at this example from informal conversation:

> … just because that's how life and friendships work and *develop* and relationships you drift in you drift out. BNC2014 (Spoken)

Develop here is a verb. In the next example, we see the noun *development*:

> Explain the attraction between Tess and Angel Clare, and how their situation at the dairy farm contributes to the *development* of their relationship. Year 8 English assessment.

Because *development* is a noun that stems from a verb, and it describes a process or action, it is called a **nominalisation**.

Other examples are *findings* in:

> Can you explain and justify your *findings?* Year 7 Maths worksheet.

as opposed to the more conversational 'what you found'.

Nominalisation is a well-known feature of many academic registers. It can be difficult to process when you are reading or listening – the natural way to describe an action is by using a verb, so using a noun instead seems odd if you are not used to it. Nominalisation is much rarer in everyday language. When we compared KS3 with KS2, a greater percentage of key words in KS3 were nouns compared to words in KS2, due to nominalisation. Research has shown that nominalised forms are associated with less good performance and comprehension in Maths.[6] It is part of the disciplinary register, so needs to be learned, but it's important to appreciate the processing difficulties it can present for some students.

Mary Schleppegrell wrote that 'a key challenge in mathematics teaching is to help students move from everyday, informal ways of construing knowledge into the technical and academic ways that are necessary for disciplinary learning in all subjects'[7] p. 140. What we have found suggests that a very sharp switch is expected at the primary-secondary transition. In Chapter 7, we write more about how this can be handled with students.

English

There is much less written in the academic literature about the language and vocabulary of school English, compared to Maths and Science, which have been studied by many educational linguists. There are also several studies of the language of school History and Geography, but little or nothing about English. Perhaps it is assumed that the language of learning English in school is not problematic. We do not completely agree – as we'll show, while KS3 English does not seem to have so many highly technical terms as other disciplines, it has its own unique approach, which is not conceptually simple.

In Chapter 4, we presented the Key Words of KS2 compared to KS3. This showed that the words used in English classes to describe grammar, spelling and punctuation, such as *adverbial, comma, clause, verb* and so on are so common that they dominated the word list for our whole KS2 corpus. Obviously, this is due to the emphasis on KS2 SATs in English.

With KS2 SATs behind, KS3 English begins to focus even more strongly on the study of literature, and our key word studies suggested to us that the goals of the discipline of English in secondary school have stepped up significantly from those of KS2. We are not sure whether the goals are actually articulated to students out loud. In the rush of starting secondary school, it would not be surprising if some students don't grasp that the goals have changed, unless this is pointed out to them very clearly. This will increase the challenge of the new texts they are studying.

Tables 4.5 and 4.6 give the top 30 key words of KS3 compared to KS2, and vice versa. As before, words related to class management, and words repeated on headers and footers have been deleted. This search also turned up a lot of names of fictional characters and features of the landscape of literature, especially in KS3, which we have left out of the lists.

We wrote in the previous chapter that the words of KS2 English are overwhelmingly focused on the aspects of language that are tested in the English SATs.

Table 4.5 Key Words in KS3 English compared to KS2 English

Analysis	Develop	Feature	Important	Supernatural
Annotate	Discuss	Genre	Poem	Technique
Attitude	Effect	Gothic	Poetry	Tension
Audience	Evidence	Historical	Quotation	Theme
Comment	Explore	Idea	Reader	Tone
Create	Fear	Identity	Structure	Writer

Table 4.6 Key Words in KS2 English compared to KS3 English

Adverbial	Co-ordinate	Instruction	Preposition	Root
Antonym	Embed	Opener	Pronoun	Semi-colon
Bracket	Ending	Parenthesis	Punctuate	Subjunctive
Clause	Expanded	Passive	Relative	Subordinate
Comma	Exclamation	Plural	Report	Suffix
Conjunction	Hyphen	Prefix	Rewrite	Version

The fact that these show up as key words against KS3 shows that they are much rarer or, in some cases, not used at all after the transition to secondary school.

There are some interesting themes in the KS3 Key Word list which we'll discuss now.

Critiquing texts in KS3

We looked at examples of all the KS3 key words listed, and tried to work out how they are used and what main themes they express. Our first theme is expressed through the words in Box 4.3.

Box 4.3   Words that are used to express the choices made by writers

attitude create effect explore historical technique tone writer

---

These words seem to direct students to think about the choices that writers made as they wrote. Here are examples:

Create
Think specifically about the atmosphere *created*. Year 8 presentation

How does Dickens *create* Miss Haversham's character in this extract? Year 7 presentation.

effect
What sort of *effect* is Armitage aiming for? Year 8 worksheet.

explore
What ideas about rural and urban life do these extracts *explore*? Year 8 assessment.

writer
Think about the agenda behind the song: what does the *writer* want people to think/ feel as a reaction to this song? Year 7 presentation.

Reading these and many other examples, we came to see that what holds them together is a view of the text – book, extract, play, poem, etc. – as the result of a series of choices that the writer made. The text that exists, that we are reading, could be thought of alongside the possible, imaginary texts that could have been created if different choices had been made at each step of the way. Students are encouraged to consider these choices, the writer's motives in making them, and to evaluate them.

The reading experience

The previous theme was about the writer and the choices they made. Very closely related to this is the reader and their experience as they read the text, and some of the same words are used. Every text is written in a particular context, historical and social, for a particular purpose and with an intended effect on the reader. To do well, students are encouraged to articulate their experience of reading, the emotional effects they experience, and how they might respond to a text.

attitude

> How would a modern audience respond to the *attitudes* reflected in this passage? Year 8 assessment.

audience

> Shakespeare shows how vulnerable Macbeth is and reminds the *audience* how changed he is since his 'valour' and 'lion' like behaviour at the start of the play. Year 7 presentation.

reader

> What action in the opening line might make the *reader* feel tense? Year 8 presentation.

These two related themes seems to us to be a development from the kind of literary analysis that Year 6 students have to do for their KS2 English Reading paper. The new demands reflect the KS3 curriculum, and ultimately the disciplinary goals of studying literature at an advanced level. Currently for the KS2 reading assessment, children have to read three short texts from different genres. They have to show comprehension by answering factual questions about the text. They also have to infer; for example, why a character was nervous, or surprised. There are questions about the meanings of words and phrases, in which children have to show understandings of lower frequency words, such as *wriggled* and *vulnerable* (2023 test), by selecting the best synonym or explanation from a list. Some of what seem to us to be the most demanding questions require students to choose the best way of summarising key messages in the text, from a list of options. What students are **not** usually asked to do is to critique the text holistically, in the round, (though we recognise that some KS2 teachers start working with texts in this way, especially in the time after SATs). Thinking of texts in this way is seeing them as artefacts, defined in the Oxford Learners' Dictionary as 'an object that is made by a person, especially something of historical or cultural interest'.

Analysing and creating texts in KS3

The frequency of words like *structure* shows that students now have to focus on text at the organisational level of discourse, rather than looking at grammar within the sentence, or word meaning. Students are directed to consider the structure of the texts that they read, as well as to think about how they structure their own writing.

> You just moved ahead a bit too quickly guys you're missing out some parts of the *structure* of the story. Year 7 teacher talk.

> Aim to keep your story brief but to *structure* it well. Year 8 presentation.

There is consideration of *genre*, and its *features*:

> How do other writers use gothic *features* to create fear? Year 8 presentation.

In terms of the tasks expected of them, these examples show that KS3 students are being inducted into the register of literary discussion and criticism. This is a contrast with the mostly more reactive, responsive KS2 tasks. We can see examples of this in the very frequent words *evidence* and *quotation*:

> We've discussed a number of quotes that you could put into your *evidence*. Year 7 teacher talk.

> Organising this kind of structured response to a piece of literature is a step up from the KS2 SAT tasks of responding to specific prompts.

Literary themes

Finally, there are some big personal, emotional and societal themes in KS3; *theme* itself is a frequent word. A central one is *identity*, which we found 178 times in KS3, where it was often a theme in studying poetry. In comparison, the KS2 corpus had only eight examples (some in the phrase *identity cards*). A KS3 example is:

> He often writes and speaks about cultural *identity*, concerning race and nationality. Year 7 presentation.

Other emotions and themes that come up are *family*, *fear*, *hardship*, *horror*, *power*, *death*, *marriage* and *war*.

Science

An old-fashioned view of school Science was that it was for the scientists of the future. It was the first step of the training that leads to the white coat in the laboratory or the Physics calculations on the dusty university chalkboard. These days, most educators agree that Science should be for everyone. It is part of the essential life knowledge we should all have, to understand personal issues such as substance use, nutrition and reproductive health, and societal challenges like climate change and the growth of antibiotic resistant infections. The language of Science is probably the most studied out of all of the school subject registers. Researchers agree that children need to learn scientific language to be able to access scientific concepts and to think like a scientist.[8] In short, we all need Science, and we need scientific language to understand it.

The size of new vocabulary in Science

One of the earliest articles about the vocabulary of school Science was published in 1987, by Gottfried Merzyn.[9] He calculated that in his context, Germany, students are introduced to more new words in every Science lesson than in each of their foreign language lessons – around 2,000 words per year. This seems very surprising, but what we found from our word lists showed that it is not as unbelievable as it sounds. In Chapter 3, we described key words from KS3 compared to KS2. We found that these were mostly dominated by Science words. Here, we first present the key words of KS3, then look briefly at the biggest issue in the registers of school Science, multiple meanings, which is covered in more depth in the next chapter. The top 30 Science key words for KS3 compared to KS2 and vice versa are given in Tables 4.7 and 4.8, with class management words omitted.

Table 4.7 Key Words in KS3 Science compared to KS2 Science

Acid	Combustion	Element	Magnesium	Pressure
Alkali	Compound	Equation	Mass	React
Atom	Copper	Formula	Oxide	Sodium
Calculate	Cytoplasm	Kinetic	Particle	State
Chloride	Decrease	Hydrochloric	Periodic	Transfer
Chloroplast	Electron	Hydrogen	Potassium	Zinc

Table 4.8 Key Words in KS2 Science compared to KS3 Science

Adaptive	Butterfly	Evolution	Micro-organism	Shark
Amphibian	Charles	Galapagos	Minibeast	Trait
Ancestor	City	Jellyfish	Photograph	Vertebrate
Antenna	Creature	Invention	Plastic	Whale
Beak	Darwin	Invertebrate	Reptile	Wing
Believe	Decay	Mammal	Shadow	Worm

Nouns and narratives

We can see straightaway that both sets of key words have a lot of nouns in them, but of very different kinds. The KS3 nouns are mostly words for elements (e.g. *copper*, *magnesium*) and compounds, while the KS2 nouns are mostly animals or parts of animals.

The KS2 words *charles*, *darwin* and *believe*, as well as some just outside the top 30, *Edison*, *Newton* and *Marie*, tell us something about the register of KS2 Science. As you can see, most of these are names of scientists: Charles Darwin, Edison, Newton, and Marie Curie (who writers tended to refer to as Marie, rather than by her surname as for the male scientists). This is a reflection of the narrative style of a lot of the KS2 Science texts. Here are some examples:

> After some tests and changes, *Edison* created a lightbulb that would stay lit using electricity for 13 1/2 hours! Year 6 worksheet.

> When he went ashore, *Darwin* found plants and animals that nobody had seen before. Year 6 presentation.

believe is also part of narratives:

> Until the 19th century, people *believed* that diseases were caused by all sorts of strange things including the gods and the stars! Year 6 textbook.

> He heard that local people *believed* that they wouldn't catch smallpox if they'd already had another disease called cowpox. Year 6 textbook.

Many texts in KS2 Science tell the stories of discoveries, with the scientist as the star of the narrative. We are told what people believed before, rightly or wrongly, and often the story of discovery includes something unexpected which leads to the scientist having a 'lightbulb' moment of insight. This is a different way of organising text from professional science texts, which focus on processes and keep the human scientist in the background.[10] The following KS3 examples are typical in that the subject (underlined) is not a human but rather a scientific concept. They're in the present tense because they tell us something about the way the scientific world is. This is in contrast with the KS2 sentences above, which are in the past tense, because they tell part of a story of a discovery.

> Pressure is a measure of how much force is applied over a certain area. Year 8 textbook.

> Some energy is also transferred to the surroundings if the gas is turned off and the water is then left to cool down. Year 8 presentation.

The KS3 Science register is closer to expert registers, in its focus on scientific processes rather than the human scientist. As for the other subjects we've discussed,

Table 4.9 Examples of words used in KS3 Science and in everyday language

word	KS3 example	Everyday language
Pressure	The *pressure* inside the container increases. (Year 7 textbook)	His team struggled in the face of *pressure*.
Equation	You can calculate weight using an *equation*. (Year 7 textbook)	… Take him out of the *equation* because he's the new kid on the block.
Solid	Iodine is a brittle *solid* at room temperature. (Year 8 textbook)	The acting is very *solid* throughout.
Image	This magnifies the *image* using lenses. (Year 7 textbook)	… His clean *image* as a player'
Substance	… Separating an insoluble *substance* from a soluble one. (Year 8 teacher talk)	There was nothing of *substance*.

the students are being inducted into the disciplinary register, but again, there is a fairly sharp switch of focus at the beginning of KS3.

Multiple meanings in Science

As we examined the full list of specialist words in Science, we realised that a major issue is words that have different meanings in everyday language from their Science ones. We'll discuss this across KS3 in the next chapter, and Appendix 2 gives a longer list. In Table 4.9, we give some examples from a key word comparison between KS3 Science and everyday language.

What struck us about all of these pairs of meanings was that the meaning in Science is very exact and precise. The meaning in everyday language is quite often metaphorical. We talk about psychological *pressure* or *stress* in everyday language, but about literal, measurable and concrete *pressure* in Science. *Solid* in everyday language often means 'good, reliable', as opposed to its meaning of 'not liquid or gas' in Science. An *image* in Science is something that you can literally see, whereas in everyday language it may mean a social perception. This is an aspect of multiple meaning that is particularly pronounced in Science.

History

We have less data for History and Geography, because there was less available from our contributing schools. This is a reflection of the amount of class time spent on the different subjects. It was particularly tricky to get texts from KS2 partly because of the dominance of Maths and English in preparation for SATs, and also because the subjects were sometimes covered as part of holistic topics rather than as named subjects. We did get enough to find key words but these can't be seen as necessarily representative of all schools.

A few researchers have looked at the language of school History, but have tended to focus on textbooks, and not in the UK context. Textbooks are not a big part of our corpora, which we compiled following what the participating schools told us about the materials that they used. All the same, we found some interesting points that previous researchers had made about the goals of history: Schleppegrell and her colleagues write that historians 'arrange, interpret and generalise from facts and events',[11] and, in doing so, they de-emphasise individual people. This may mark a change similar to that in Science, where KS3 moves away from narrative accounts. We looked at the key words to see if this is borne out. Tables 4.10 and 4.11 show the key words from KS3 compared to KS2 and vice versa.

Key words in KS3 and KS2 history

We can see that the KS2 words are virtually all associated with specific topics that students are learning about in History in our partner schools. These were: The Egyptians, South America, the invention of the railway and the industrial age, the Vikings. We also checked the KS2 corpus against everyday English and found very similar key words. We only had data from eight primary schools and it is very

Table 4.10 Key Words in KS3 History compared to KS2 History

Abolition	Communist	Evidence	Peasant	Revolutionise
Agree	Continuity	Factor	Plantation	Rival
Attitude	Contribute	Freedom	Portrait	Significant
Change	Control	Independence	Rebellion	Slavery
Claim	Empire	Interpretation	Reform	Sources
Colony	Enslave	Judgement	Relatively	Violence

Table 4.11 Key Words in KS2 History compared to KS3 History

Afterlife	Falcon	Lighthouse	Passenger	Railway
Ancient	Goddess	Linen	Persian	Tomb
Axis	Greeks	Locomotive	Pharaoh	Tutankhamun
Chocolate	Hitler	Mayan	Poppy	Underworld
Colliery	Jar	Organ	Pyramid	Viking
Egyptian	Kraken	Osiris	Ra	Wrap

likely that other schools were covering different topics. We expect that while the exact words might be different, we would still find very theme based vocabulary if we looked at other schools.

Topics and themes in KS3 key words

Like the KS2 words, some of the KS3 key words are associated with the topics studied in our partner schools. These were the British empire and royalty, and the history and abolition of slavery. The associated words include *abolition, claim* (to the throne), *colony, empire, enslave, peasant, plantation, slavery*.

Secondly, in addition to these topic-related words, there were also words associated with broader historical themes and topics. There are several words around change (or lack of): *change, continuity, reform, revolutionise*.

> Peterloo is a critical event [...] because ultimately it *changed* public opinion to influence the extension of the right to vote. Year 8 presentation.

> More *reform* acts had given more men the right to vote. Year 8 presentation.

Thirdly, there is a group related to fighting for control or freedom, linked to the slavery and empire themes but appearing across the corpus. These include *control, freedom, independence, rebellion, violence*.

> Therefore Britain had to keep *control* not just of the seas themselves but of the island. Year 8 presentation.

> ... he wanted to grant religious *freedom* in England. Year 8 reading extract.

Skills in KS3 key words

Some of the KS3 key words are associated with the specific skills associated with the discipline, such as evaluating and interpreting sources and evidence. In our key words, these were: *agree, attitude, evidence, interpretation, judgement, portrait* (a specific type of source), source.

> An *interpretation* is something that was written about an event by someone who didn't experience it first hand. Year 7 presentation.

> Choose a sentence you *agree* with and be prepared to explain why. Year 7 presentation.

> What *evidence* of a revolution can you spot? Year 8 presentation.

> How does it show a changing *attitude* towards empire? Year 8 teacher talk.

Other words are associated with tracing relationships between events and ideas, often of cause/ effect or comparison. In our top 30, these words are *contribute*, *factor*, *significant*.

> African resistance to enslavement and kidnapping *contributed* to growing public support and opposition to slave trafficking. Year 8 reading extract.

> The key to understanding this question is by looking at three important *factors*: trade, war and exploration. Year 8 textbook,

> Why was Captain Cook so *significant* for the growing British Empire? Year 8 worksheet.

In KS3 History then, we see that central historical themes and skills are being developed. There is still a narrative component to much of the text, but less so than in KS2. There is also an increasing emphasis on social, group actions and movements, and corresponding decrease in narratives of the lives of individuals.

Geography

Research has repeatedly found that like other school subjects, Geography has its own register, with specialist meanings of words, and that geographical skills are interdependent with literacy of the Geography register.[12] Peter Wignell and colleagues wrote that the language of Geography has developed for three purposes.[13] Firstly, at the most basic level, there are words and specialist terminology to explain in detail what we can see in the world, our observations. Secondly, words help to organise or classify what we observe, and thirdly to try to explain it. We looked at the key words of KS3 against KS2 and vice versa to see if there was evidence of these purposes, or other patterns. Our top 30s are in Tables 4.12 and 4.13.

KS3 and KS2 key words

The Geography corpora are very small, so these lists should be taken as very general indications of what is happening. We can see a similar pattern to other subjects,

Table 4.12 Key Words in KS3 Geography compared to KS2 Geography

Adaptation	Decline	Effect	Natural	Seasonal
Axis	Development	Graph	Population	Site
Billion	Die	Lack	Physical	Slum
Birth	Economic	Location	Rate	Sparse
Climate	Ecosystem	Migration	Resident	Strategy
Conflict	Environment	Model	Scale	Tourism

Table 4.13 Key Words in KS2 Geography compared to KS3 Geography

Amazon	Course	Footbridge	Mouth	Severn
Boundary	Dam	GMT	Navigation	Stream
Chocolate	Delta	Iron (earth's crust)	Nile	Tectonic
Commerce	Discharge (verb)	Island	Peru	Thames
Compass	Fairtrade	Length	River	Tidal
Convergent	Floodplain	Mississippi	Route	Yangtze

where KS2 seems to deal with very specific topics. This leads to a lot of names and concrete nouns, in this list, names of rivers, and words associated with rivers, like *mouth, stream, tidal, dam* and *discharge* (into), and with the topic of Fairtrade.

KS3 themes

The KS3 key words tend to show much broader themes in human and physical Geography rather than the specific physical features of KS2. These include *adaptation, climate, conflict, development, environment, migration, seasonal*.

> They have evolved a number of special *adaptations* to cope with the low temperatures, strong winds and dry conditions. Year 8 presentation.

> … The lack of motorways and access to ports restricts *migration*. Year 7 teacher talk.

> .. The *seasonal* melt of the permafrost means off-road travel cannot be undertaken in the summer. Year 8 presentation.

There are also words associated with the skills and tools of studying Geography: *axis, graph, model, scale,* and with links between factors: *effect*.

> .. along the bottom *axis* we have the number of people. Year 8 teacher talk.

> Use the *scale* bar to work out the distance along the river from High Force to the bridge. Year 8 presentation.

> It measured 7 on the Richter *scale*. Year 8 presentation.

The key words in Geography give evidence of the same patterns that we saw for other subjects. In KS2 the focus is concrete and around specific entities – in Geography, these are locations and physical features, as compared with the characters and objects of KS2 History. In KS3, the key words show a focus on the major themes of the discipline, which underlie and unify the individual examples that students may already be familiar with. Again, KS3 requires a move towards abstraction and to the disciplinary goals and language that can take them through to advanced study.

Summary

In this chapter, we have shown the key words for each of the five subject disciplines we studied, with the warning that for History and Geography our datasets are quite small, so the words should be taken as indicative of general patterns, not set in stone. We looked at examples from our corpus and we have tried to trace what central ideas and perspectives these words express. We have been thinking particularly of the challenges that any new perspectives might present to students at the primary-secondary transition, where there seem to be some shifts in direction. As we have said, we would expect differences, because learning should represent progression, but we wonder whether some of the developments are quite marked at the transition. We also wondered to what extent this is made explicit, or whether students need to work out for themselves that there has been a change in the goals.

In Chapter 7, we have reduced these key word lists to the top 10 for each subject after discussion with subject teachers, and we write about how students can be supported with this language.

Notes

1 https://assets.publishing.service.gov.uk/media/661530cdc4c84d6602346a13/ccus-iccc-business-models-update-april-2024.pdf
2 Dowker, A., Sarkar, A. & Looi, C. Y. 2016. Mathematics anxiety: What have we learned in 60 years? *Frontiers in Psychology, 7*(508), pp. 1–16.
3 Cruz Neri, N. & Retelsdorf, J. 2022. The role of linguistic features in science and math comprehension and performance: A systematic review and desiderata for future research. *Educational Research Review*, 36(May), p. 100460
4 Thompson, D. & Rubenstein, R. 2000. Learning mathematics vocabulary: Potential pitfalls and learning strategies. *The Mathematics Teacher*, 93/7, pp. 568–574.
5 Candarli, D. & Oxley, F. 2023. The language of mathematics. In Deignan, A., Candarli, D. & Oxley, F. (eds.) *The linguistic challenge of the transition to secondary school*. Routledge, pp. 171–200.
6 Cruz Neri, N. & Retelsdorf, J. 2022. The role of linguistic features in science and math comprehension and performance: A systematic review and desiderata for future research. *Educational Research Review*, 36(May), p. 100460
7 Schleppegrell, M. 2007. The linguistic challenges of mathematics teaching and learning: A research review. *Reading and Writing Quarterly*, 23/2, pp. 139–159.
8 Dawes, L. 2004. Talk and learning in classroom science. *International Journal of Science Education,* 26(6), pp. 677–695; Fang, Z. 2005. Scientific literacy: A systemic functional linguistics perspective. *Science Education*, 89, pp. 335–347.
9 Merzyn, G. 1987. The language of school science. *International Journal of Science Education*, 9/4, pp. 483–489.

10 Myers, G. 1994. Narratives of science and nature in popularising molecular genetics. In Coulthard, M. (ed.) *Advances in written discourse analysis.* Routledge, pp. 193–204.

11 For example, Schleppegrell, M., Achugar, M. & Oteíza, T. 2004. The grammar of history: Enhancing content-based instruction through a functional focus on language. *TESOL Quarterly*, 38/1, pp. 67–93.

12 Heidari, N., Feser, M., Scholten, N., Schwippert, K. & Sprenger, S. 2023. Language in primary and secondary education: A systematic literature review of empirical geography education research. *International Research in Geographical and Environmental Education*, 32/3, pp. 234–251.

13 Wignell, P., Martin, J. R. & Eggins, S. 1989. The discourse of geography: Ordering and explaining the experiential world. *Linguistics and Education,* 1, pp. 359–391.

5 Polysemy
New meanings for old words
Alice Deignan

Introduction

At the beginning of the last chapter, I showed an extract of a government report about carbon capture. Among the words that were tricky to me were *analogue* in 'as a stable *analogue* to the carbon market price', and *exposure*, in 'an Emitter's carbon price *exposure*'. Look at examples of these words from the BNC and BNC2014 Spoken corpora:

> … an old fashioned *analogue* watch and a chunky bracelet on the right wrist. BNC.

> Being an *analogue* technology in an increasingly digital world is a drawback. BNC.

> … that's what he put it down to, *exposure* to the language. BNC2014 Spoken.

> … the risks of *exposure* to radiation. BNC.

I'm taking the BNC and BNC2014 Spoken corpora as representative of my experience of non-specialist English, and these examples from them are meanings of *analogue* and *exposure* that I am reasonably confident of. Knowing these meanings didn't help me understand the government report though, and this chapter explores why this is, and what this might mean for students.

In the last chapter, we showed that as our students progress up a specialist disciplinary curriculum, they are faced with a vast amount of new words and other language features. In this chapter, we take a close look at word meaning, and how this could cause problems for school students. We'll show how some words have an academic, school meaning that is different from its everyday meaning. When students try to use their knowledge of the everyday meaning, they sometimes misunderstand the subject content. We'll also show how some words have different meanings in different subject registers.

DOI: 10.4324/9781032645513-6

What is 'polysemy', and why is it a problem?

When we first started looking at the vocabulary of school, and how this changes as children go up through the years and key stages, we looked forward to being able to get 'The List' of new vocabulary that appears with each new school year. A year or so later, we were able to look at the lists that our computer programmes had generated for us, and we had talked to a lot of children about their understandings of language and the things they found difficult. We found that – like so many things in life! – things were more complicated than we had first thought. The new words were not necessarily very difficult, and the known words were not necessarily easy.

Sometimes, children told us that new, 'hard' words like *photosynthesis* looked scary but had not caused particular problems. They have one, very precise meaning, and the teacher and the materials had drawn attention to it. They learned the new concept along with the new word, not easily, but without too much confusion around the language. In contrast, sometimes apparently easy words did give problems, like *transfer*, in this interview extract. Here, a group of Year 7 students have been reading an article that contained the phrase *transfers of land*. The researcher tries to prompt the student, Aris, so she can see where the problem comes from.

ARIS: *I didn't understand transfers of land… 'cos I know what like transfers means and stuff it's like*

RESEARCHER: *what is transfer?*

ARIS: *it's like move it from one place to another*

RESEARCHER: *okay*

ARIS: *or like buy something and then like you bought it off someone and then you you transfer it to somebody else*

RESEARCHER: *and what is land?*

ARIS: *land is like well like land is like the field is a piece of land.*

It seems that Aris understands *transfer* as meaning 'move from one (physical) location to another', so he is understandably confused as to how this could possibly apply to a piece of land. Here, of course, it is the ownership of the land which is actually transferred, but this is likely to be a concept outside his experience. The British National Corpus 2014 (Spoken) examples of *transfer* mostly concern money, football players, and being taken from an airport to a holiday resort. From this and many other examples, we concluded that word meaning and use can be tricky for even easy-looking words.

When we stop to work out what a word means, we find that it is not always straightforward. Many, many words have more than one meaning. Dictionary entries can be very helpful here, as they number and define each meaning separately. The entries for many words contain quite long lists of meanings, especially for the words that are more frequently used, like *see*, *time*, or *present*. These very frequent words sometimes have dozens of related but distinguishable meanings. Rare words like *photosynthesis* tend to have just one meaning, but the more often a word is used, the more meanings it seems to have. For example, the Oxford Advanced Learners' Dictionary (online)[1] gives 18 major meanings for the word *see*. It also shows a lot of phrases, such as *seeing that* (= because of the fact that) and *see something coming*. *Present* has many meanings as a verb, including 'give', 'cause [difficulties]', 'produce', show', 'introduce' and so on. It also has meanings as an adjective, in phrases like *the present situation* and *the dust was present everywhere*. These are all quite formal and abstract meanings. However, for school students, probably by far the most immediate and familiar meaning of *present* is the noun meaning 'gift'. The technical linguistic term for words having multiple meanings is 'polysemy'.

Box 5.1 Polysemy

Polysemy means 'many meanings' (from the Ancient Greek poly = 'many', 'sem'= sign). **Polysemy** describes the general idea of multiple meanings. Words that have more than one meaning are described as being **polysemous**. An example of a polysemous word is *heated*. The different meanings can be seen in these examples:

… a *heated* indoor pool.

'…a *heated* debate.

We can see that the meanings are related to each other, but the first one has a physical reference and the second refers to emotions. Most people would consider them to be different meanings of the same word, but there are no hard and fast rules. It is about perception.

You many have heard the term 'homonym'. **Homonyms** are words which are technically different, but have the same spelling and sound. A classic example of a pair of homonyms is *bank*, for example:

…walking along the *bank* of the Thames.

…how much money does he have in the *bank*?

Linguists often look at the history of words to decide if they are homonyms, homonyms being words which have different origins or histories. (River) *bank* comes via the Old Norse for 'bench'. (Financial) *bank* comes via the Italian for 'table', referring to money changers' tables. If we go back far enough, they are the same word, but history has led to them having very different meanings.

As far as we are concerned in this book, whether a word is polysemous (*heated*), or two homonyms (*bank*) is not important. That is a theoretical debate, and what matters here is whether the word meanings might be confusing for students.

In Chapter 1, we explained how we had used computer software tools to count words in different contexts, comparing early secondary school language data with late primary and everyday language. Computer tools like this are incredibly helpful to the language researcher and teacher. They give us reliable information that it would be almost impossible to work out by hand. However, computers do not (yet!) understand language, and they cannot tell us what words mean. To work out the meanings of words, human insight is needed.

While we know that words often have many meanings, they don't have a fixed number that can be explained in a definitive list. Rosamund Moon,[2] a researcher and expert lexicographer, wrote that there are 'no final or absolute answers' to the question of how many meanings any word has (p. 86). Word meanings shade into each other, and what we count as a different meaning can depend on our purpose – whether we're writing a detailed specialist dictionary, or just explaining an idea to a friend for example. It is quite common for someone to know some meanings of a word, but be less familiar with others. For example, I could confidently use and define the word *security* when it is used to talk about a feeling of safety, but I would not try to describe its technical meaning in economics, because I only have a vague understanding of it.

To give an example of how polysemy might be a challenge to school students, think about the meaning of *release* in the following sentences. These were taken from materials intended for primary and early secondary school:

When fossil fuels are burned, the carbon that has been trapped inside them for millions of years is *released* into the atmosphere as carbon dioxide.

from BBC Bitesize Key Stage 2 Learn and Revise 'Climate change'

Burning the rainforest *releases* CO_2, which contributes to world climate change.

from a powerpoint presentation for a Year 8 geography class.

Box 5.2 Practical suggestion

Even though we use words with their general and academic meanings every day, it is very difficult to work out what meanings they have when you just sit down to think about it in the abstract. Online dictionaries can provide a very quick shortcut and some helpful examples. The websites for *Oxford Learners' Dictionaries*, *Cambridge Learner Dictionaries*, *Longman Dictionary of Contemporary English* and others give very clear lists of meanings. I prefer these learner dictionaries because they tackle the everyday meanings. Other kinds of dictionaries focus on 'hard' or rare meanings, or the history of words, which are not relevant here.

If you want to explore word meaning and use in more depth, you could look directly at the British National Corpus, as we described in Chapter 1. That is much more time consuming, and we would only recommend it if you have a particular research interest or want to explore the vocabulary area in depth.

This might seem to be a completely straightforward meaning to us, as adults. We have probably seen thousands of examples of *release* used in this way, and we bring a lot of background knowledge to the task of interpreting the word. However, this meaning is not quite the same as any of the everyday meanings of *release*, described by the *Oxford Advanced Learners' Dictionary* (online) as:

> to let somebody come out of a place where they have been kept or stuck and unable to leave or move
>
> *The hostages were released unharmed.*
>
> *He was released without charge after questioning by police.*
>
> to make a film, recording or other product available to the public
>
> *He's planning to release a solo album.*
>
> *They've released a new version of the original film.*

These meanings of *release* describe something deliberate, done by humans. The 'climate' meaning describes a process. It is an unintentional side effect of burning, and it is almost always used about carbon dioxide. In the BNC, the 'climate' meaning of *release* is rare, relative to the everyday meanings. When we looked at a random sample of examples, we found that it only accounts for about 0.5% of the total uses of the word. This means that it is quite possible that some of our students might not have come across this 'climate' meaning before, especially students who are less regularly exposed to science and current affairs language outside the classroom.

As literate adults, we can easily see a relationship between the various meanings of *release*, without even thinking consciously about it. We can use all these meanings without problems. It isn't as easy for less experienced language users like our students. A few years ago, our team interviewed groups of secondary school students about their understanding of climate change. The young people we interviewed had all studied the subject in science and geography and had a basic understanding of the carbon cycle. Some students articulated their understanding very well. However, when they described it to us, they rarely used *release* in the technical way. Instead, they described the process using other words. For example, a Year 10 student told us:

> And like the fossil fuels, we're burning like loads of it, is causing lots of carbon dioxide levels to increase and pollution is like increasing in the world as well.

One Year 9 student used *release* in talking about the causes of climate change, but we were not convinced that he had a good command of this meaning. We thought that he had probably noticed the word from his reading or his teacher's explanation, but did not really understand the way it is used in the language of science. He told us:

> [the blanket of gases is] getting thicker because erm, there's more pollutants and they're like carbon dioxide, so cos it's getting thicker, less oxygen, over less gases, like bounce back off. So they're getting less *released* so there's holes in there, which makes it more, er warmer.

Another Year 9 student said

> If we're recycling stuff like the landfills, I don't know, it *releases* something like, you know, less landfills and less pollution and stuff like that.

Again, we thought that this student probably did not have a precise understanding of the scientific meaning of *release*. Both the teachers and the students involved would probably assume that *release* is a word that all KS3 and KS4 students would know. They are right – but while the students most likely know the two everyday meanings of *release* very well, many of them will only have a hazy grasp of the scientific meaning, and will avoid using it themselves. This problem is possibly made worse because nobody actually realises that it is a problem.

This issue of polysemy between everyday meanings and academic ones has been noticed by many education writers and teachers. Ziuhui Fang[3] writes about the US school context and the difficulties that students face with the language of their academic texts. He analysed two science textbooks widely used in the schools where he taught 11–14-year-olds. One of the major issues he noticed was ordinary words which also have specialist meanings. He writes: 'Words like *school*, *fault* and *volume* are common in children's everyday vocabulary' (p. 494), but that they also have specialist scientific meanings. His examples are:

> Fishes that swim in *schools* are often safer than fishes that swim alone, because it is harder for predators to see and select an individual fish.

> How rocks move along a *fault* depends on how much friction there is between the opposite sides of the fault.

> A liter is a measurement of liquid *volume*.

Fang writes that words like this can be particularly difficult because students can decode them, 'but the meanings that they assign to these words often do not enable them to comprehend successfully' (p. 494).

We think that in some ways, words with multiple meanings can be even more difficult for students than purely technical words. This is because often neither the students nor the teachers necessarily realise that the academic meaning of the word is new. Everybody is busy, there are many other new words, and a familiar-looking word does not always get a second glance. Sometimes though, its academic, subject-specific meaning might be very important. We found this problem with many students who we spoke to. We asked some Year 7 students if they had found any words difficult as they started secondary school, and one group told us about problems with the word *significant*.

ELLIE: *this one time this question was really hard for all of us 'cos we haven't learnt this word it was significant.*

JAKE: *yeah significant and now oh yeah and now like I get it so I know what it means.*

INTERVIEWER: *mhm*

JAKE: *and I can do the questions.*

INTERVIEWER: *so what does it mean?*

JAKE: *it means the special number I think.*

Jake seems very confident that he knows the meaning of *significant* and says he is able to use it in answering maths questions, while Ellie is less sure.

We checked out the meaning of *significant* that the children had probably come across, by searching through our corpus of teaching materials and lesson transcripts, which their school had contributed to. In our secondary Maths corpus, we found 73 examples of *significant*. Almost all of them were followed by *figure* or *figures*. This sentence, from a powerpoint presentation, helps us to get an idea of the meaning:

> When you are rounding to decimal places, you start counting after the decimal point, but with *significant* figures, you start counting at the first non-zero number.

Our corpus also contained also a lot of assessment questions, such as

> Round the following to one *significant* figure.

Jake's understanding of *significant* as meaning 'special number' won't be adequate to help him tackle this question, despite his confidence. He would be interpreting the question as 'round to one special number', and is unlikely to get the answer right. He will be puzzled by this as he is sure he knows what the question means.

So, where did he get the definition 'special number' from? Our search of current, everyday English showed that it has a wide range of uses, mostly meaning something like 'important', or 'major', such as *significant threat*, and *significant increase*. One use, which is concerned with numbers, and which might be heard by students in their family context is *significant birthday*. Typical examples from real-life, non-school contexts are:

> She has a *significant birthday* coming up uh twenty ninth January. BNC2014 Spoken.

> ... a great holiday and a very special way to celebrate a *significant birthday*. English web TenTen corpus.

Jake's definition of 'the special number' fits this use of *significant* very well, and he might have heard it in connection with a family member's birthday; perhaps his mother or father had a round-number birthday recently. On the one hand, it is very positive that he is using his everyday word-knowledge constructively to try to understand the language of school. Unfortunately though, this definition might not help him with the much more specific meaning needed for his Maths assessments.

In another interview, Year 7 students were confused about the meaning of *concentration*. They had read a reading extract for Year 7 Science, about cells and diffusion, which contained this sentence:

> Diffusion is the movement of particles from a place where they are in a high *concentration* to a place where they are in a low concentration.

There was some explanation of what this meant, in terms which we, as adults, thought were clear. The project researcher asked groups of children what they understood by various words in the extract, including *concentration*.

RESEARCHER: *what does concentration mean in this text?*

DAVID: *it means to like focus...*

KHALID: *I think I know what that means..*

NINA: *[whispering] What does it mean?*

KHALID: *It means to focus and you're not distracted.*

NINA: *it's just that when it says concentration we always think it's the concentration like focus and everything.*

THOMAS: *yeah.*

NINA: *but there's also different meanings of it.*

THOMAS: *it's where the Naz it's where the Nazis put people*

We can see in this extract that the children immediately think of the 'think hard' meaning of *concentration*, even though they have just read examples of the scientific meaning. As they realise that this meaning does not work here, Thomas remembers the work they have been covering in English about *concentration* **camps**. This meaning, of course, is also irrelevant here. Of the 30 children who were interviewed (in six groups), only one child was able to give the correct meaning from this context:

RESEARCHER: *okay and what is concentration?*

MARY: *in this text it means like they've got it's got a high group of things of like in that spot at but but in like other pla= in learning like I forgot in a learning perspective it means getting on with your work and not really stopping but you get along you get you get on with it and I don't know*

> **Box 5.3   Teaching implication**
>
> Encouraging students to work out meanings and apply their background knowledge is generally useful, helping them to develop independent vocabulary learning strategies. However, we need to bear in mind that academic meanings might be much more specific than the everyday ones they already know. From a student's point of view, the new meanings are not always guessable.
>
> Think about whether it might be more helpful to explicitly compare the two meanings by asking questions like:
>
> 'Have you seen this word before?' 'What does it mean to you?'
>
> 'What do you think it means here?' (showing examples of the academic use)
>
> 'Is it the same or different as the meaning you knew already?'
>
> 'How is it different?'

CHILDREN: *[laughing]*

RESEARCHER: *but in this text*

MARY: *it's a like it's a high group like there's a lot of things there like there's a concentration so there's much more things there than is in an another space*

Even here, the 'think hard' meaning is the one that is mentioned first. Mary's explanation of the scientific meaning suggests that she is not very confident of it. She is more or less repeating the text that is in front of them.

As described in Chapter 1, we analysed 17 interviews with six groups of children in Years 6 and 7. The researcher never asked about polysemy explicitly, but often asked which words were difficult, or what a particular word in a reading text meant. The problem of polysemy cropped up in 116 places across the interviews. This was either because the children said the word was a problem, or because they gave the wrong meaning of a word in the text. We think therefore that this is a very widespread difficulty. It tends not to get noticed in the normal day-to-day activity of the classroom, unless a child makes a really obvious mistake. Teachers do not usually have the time to probe understandings in the way that our researcher did.

Another difficulty with polysemy is that a lot of the academic meanings of words are abstract, which makes them harder. A recent piece of research[4] found that more 'imageable' words or meanings or words are easier for children to learn. For example, '*cycle* as in ride a bicycle is more "imageable" than *cycle* as in recurring process' (p. 293), which would make it easier to learn and remember – as well as, of course, it being much more likely to be within students' direct experience.

The discussion of polysemy in the research literature first started with the language of Science. We found that it seems to be a particular problem there, and Chapter 4 we gave some more examples. However, polysemy is found in words in all academic subjects. Peter Wignell and his colleagues[5] studied the academic language of Geography. They wrote that some technical terms, like *environment*, are taken from everyday language and mean essentially the same. In the school context however, the use is much more technical and narrow. Mathematics education researchers Thompson and Rubenstein[6] produced a detailed list of difficulties that students face in learning the vocabulary of Maths, discussed in the previous chapter. The first on their list reads 'Some words are shared by mathematics and everyday English but they have distinct meanings'. Their examples include: *prime*, *power*, *domain*, *mode*, and *imaginary* (p. 569). We explored the problem in our corpus of school materials from Years 5 to 8, and describe what we found in the next section.

Polysemy in our corpus

So many teachers and researchers have come across the problem of polysemy that we were convinced it must be very widespread. However, the examples that the writers give are words that they have noticed as part of their teaching, or they have found through detailed reading of textbooks. That was enough to show that polysemy is common, but it doesn't tell us exactly how common, or what the most problematic words might be, in which subjects. This is where our corpus can help. At the beginning of this chapter, we wrote that our computer software cannot understand or tell us about meaning. What it can tell us though, is what the most frequent words are in a year or key stage, or a subject. We compared these words with everyday language, and with the language from earlier academic years. This helped us to draw up a list of the words that are likely to be new to students, or are much more frequent in a particular subject, or year/key stage. We then studied examples of these words in use, to see just how widespread polysemy is.

What we found was that polysemy is incredibly frequent, across all the subjects that we looked at. It ranges from meanings that are completely different, through meanings that are similar but more detailed in the secondary school texts, to meanings that look quite similar, but appear in different contexts. Even words that seem very similar in meaning can be confusing when a student meets them in a different context. This is a bit like bumping into someone who we know slightly but in a different situation from usual – sometimes, we know that we know the person, but we find it difficult to recall their name or how it is we know them. We give some examples here.

Examples of most common polysemous words from our corpora

Box 5.4 shows the most common KS3 words that have slightly different meanings in school academic subjects from everyday language. This does not mean that the school meaning is never found in everyday language, or that the everyday meaning is never found in school language. It means that we found that the dominant,

> **Box 5.4   A practical question**
>
> Words like *tension* and *pressure* have literal, physical meanings, which tend to be seen in science, and abstract, psychological meanings, often in English, or History. If you see the 'psychological' meaning, think about whether it would be difficult for students. If you think it would be difficult, would it help to compare it to the literal meaning?

Table 5.1 Top 30 most frequent polysemous words in KS3

Atmosphere	Evidence	Independent	Pressure	Symbol
Circuit	Expand	Label	Property	Tension
Current	Explore	Mass	React/reaction	Tissue
Device	Factor	Material	Solution	Variable
Element	Force (noun)	Pattern	Store	Value
Energy	Function	Plot	Substance	Volume

most frequently used meanings in our KS3 corpus were different from the most frequently used on in the BNC and BNC2014 Spoken (Table 5.1).

You'll notice that a lot of these seem to have Science meanings. We found that polysemy is very common for Science. Here are some examples of the different meanings of these words in different corpora.

Force

In everyday language, the noun *force* is mostly found in expressions like:

armed forces, police force, security force, task force, work force.

In KS3 language, it has a technical scientific meaning.

The gravitational *force* pulls in the direction towards the centre of the Earth. Year 8 Science worksheet.

… now the size of the arrow needs to represent the size of the *force*. Year 7 Science teacher talk.

Store

The most common KS3 meaning of the noun *store* is found in Science, and means a reserve, usually of energy.

The surroundings' thermal *store* of energy increases… Year 8 Science teacher talk.

In everyday language, a *store* is a shop. There is a connection between the meanings, but this might not be obvious to a student.

They can be found in most department *stores* and kitchen accessory shops. BNC.

Property

In the KS3 texts, *property* tends to mean a 'characteristic'.

… we just needed to finish off a bit of work on the chemical *properties* and the physical properties of the group one elements. Year 7 Science teacher talk.

In everyday language, a *property* is a building or estate, and a person's property is something that belongs to them.

… to prevent fire spreading from your house to your neighbour's *property*. BNC.
I rang Lost Property first thing. BNC.

Volume

The KS3 examples of *volume* tend to refer to the capacity of a three dimensional shape, in Maths, or a part of the body, in biology.

Both cuboids below have the same *volume*. Year 7 Maths worksheet.
… calculate your own lung *volume* by breathing as hard as you can into a 3 litre bottle of water. Year 7 science textbook.

In everyday language, the most common meaning is 'loudness'.

turn the *volume* down.

Explore

In KS3, especially English, *explore* is almost always abstract, meaning to try out different ideas, in an unstructured way.

We're going to be *exploring* why poetry is important and all the different aspects of poetry that we perhaps don't always consider. Year 8 English teacher talk.

In everyday language, the abstract meaning is found, but more often, the meaning is literal:

It's just a really good place to *explore* that part of the world you know.

We give more examples from this list of polysemous words in Appendix 2. Taken separately, it seems likely that none of these would cause a big problem, but as we have seen elsewhere, new words and meanings do not come along on their own. They cluster, and are part of a bigger picture that is busy and complicated, with new ideas and other stresses and strains on students.

Words that have different meanings in different school subjects

To make things even more complicated, words sometimes have different meanings across subjects. Alex Quigley[7],[8] gives examples of words which have everyday meanings as well as academic ones. For example, he writes that in everyday language, *depression* describes a low emotional state, while in Geography it is a physical landscape feature, and in History, the Great Depression was a historical period. From our study, these are some of the most common KS3 words that have different meanings in different subjects, together with examples. Some of these have other meanings in everyday language, so they are also in the previous list.

Compound

Compound is frequent in Science, Maths and English, and it has related meanings in the three subjects. In Science, it refers to a substance made of different elements. In Maths, it is used in different phrases describing things that have more than one element, or that are not simple in other ways. In English, it is used to describe a particular type of sentence, that is, one which has two parts joined with a connective and not subordinated. It was fairly easy for us to see the common element of meaning between the uses in these three subjects, but they have very specific meanings in each subject register. We think the different meanings might present problems, or require extra processing time for some students.

> … looking at what a formula is and identifying the numbers of atoms or elements in *compounds* from formulae.. Year 7 Science teacher talk.

Compound measures are measures which use more than one quantity, for example miles per gallon. Year 8 Maths presentation.

> How do we calculate area and perimeter of rectangles, triangles and *compound* shapes? Year 7 Maths presentation.

> Writers like to use a mixture of long, short, simple, *compound* and complex sentences to create different effects to make their writing interesting. Year 8 English presentation.

Tension

In Science, *tension* is used as a technical term describing a force pulling an object.

Tension is a pull that stretches an object. Compression is a push that squashes an object. Standing on a plank: *tension* or compression? Year 7 Science presentation.

In English and History, *tension* describes psychological stress. In History, the examples we found all described stress and hostility between different countries or people, but in English, it described a feeling within a person, often the reader of a book or people. The meaning in the English subject texts is not common in other subjects, and also not very common in everyday language.

There were a number of issues that created *tension* and rivalry in Europe before the First World War started. Year 8 History worksheet.

Which repeated verb in the opening two sentences might sustain this *tension* and make the reader feel nervous for our narrator? Year 8 English presentation.

This would create tension for the reader who wonders whether Beowulf can defeat such a powerful and destructive villain. Year 7 English presentation.

Pressure

Pressure has a similar pair of meanings to *tension*. In Science, Maths and Geography, it has a literal, technical meaning.

Gas particles always exert *pressure* on the walls of their container, whatever the container is made from. Year 7 Science textbook.

When they finally move an earthquake happens as the *pressure* is released. Year 8 Geography presentation.

The *pressure*, P, is inversely proportional to the volume, v. Year 7 Maths worksheet.

In English and History, *pressure* describes a psychological force. In English, this tends to act on the individual. In History, it tends to describe collective, societal forces.

What is Tess's experience here? Does she enjoy the work? What *pressures* make the work more demanding? Year 8 English assessment.

By 1884, *pressure* for political reform continued. Year 8 History reading extract.

The movement received new impetus in the early 1830s with the *pressure* created by slave rebellions. Year 8 History presentation.

Function

In Maths, *function* has a specialised, technical meaning, of a way of expressing the relationship between variables. We might occasionally use this in non-Maths language, in sentences like 'effort is a function of expected reward', but this meaning would be unusual and probably not something that KS3 students have come across. A KS3 Maths example is:

Complete the table and draw the graph for each *function*. Year 8 Maths worksheet.

In Science and English, *function* is used in a way closer to everyday language, to mean 'purpose'.

One of the *functions* of blood is to transport materials around the body. Year 7 Science worksheet.

Our next couple of lessons we're going to be learning about how the muscles and tendons and the ligaments all work together but before we do that we need to learn the other *functions* of our bones ok. Year 7 Science teacher talk.

Discuss the sentences' different *functions* and effects on the reader and how this creates tension. Year 8 English worksheet.

State

State can be a verb (as in 'state the differences') or a noun. The verb is found in assessment instructions, but we thought it was probably not a problem word or meaning. Looking at the noun, there are two main meanings in our KS3 texts: 'government/ nation', and 'condition'. These are so different that they might be thought of as homonyms (see above) rather than as an example of polysemy. As we pointed out above though, we don't think that how the meanings are labelled is very important. What matters is that they might be confusing.

We found the first meaning mostly in History, and occasionally in Geography:

Stalin believed that all farms should be owned by the *state*. Year 8 History textbook.

We found the meaning of 'condition' in Science, Geography and English:

You can compress a substance in the solid *state* because the particles touch each other. Year 7 Science textbook.

Weather is the day-to-day *state* of the air around us. Year 7 Geography presentation.

How does the narrator's emotional *state* change during the poem? Year 7 English presentation.

Although these last three examples can all be explained as 'condition', we think that the science meaning of a solid/liquid/gas state is very different in context from the way the word is used in English. This is an example of what we described above: students may recognise a word, and in theory know the meaning, but applying it in a different context can be tricky, amidst the other pressures around them in class.

We give a longer list of words that have different meanings in different subjects in Appendix 2.

Conclusion

The more we looked at examples of words, the more differences in meanings we found. Nothing that we found was completely new to us, but at the same time, we might not have realised these points on the spot, in a busy classroom. The thoughts that we have taken away from this are to be aware that students often think they know the meaning of a word because it looks familiar, but they might not actually know the meaning in a school context. Double checking is important, as are giving several examples – if in doubt, give more not less, and an online dictionary can be a very helpful way of finding these.

Notes

1 https://www.oxfordlearnersdictionaries.com/definition/english/see_1?q=see
2 Moon, R. 1987. The analysis of meaning. In Sinclair, J. (ed.) *Looking up: An account of the COBUILD project in lexical computing.* London: HarperCollins, pp. 86–103
3 Fang, Z. 2006. The language demands of science reading in middle school. *International Journal of Science Education*, 28/5, pp. 491–520.
4 Booton, S., Wonnacott, E., Hodgkiss, A., Mathers, S. & Murphy, V. 2022. Children's knowledge of multiple word meanings: Which factors count, and for whom? *Applied Linguistics*, 43/2, pp. 293–315.
5 Wignell, P., Martin, J. R. & Eggins, S. 1989. The discourse of geography. *Linguistics and Education*, 1, pp. 359–391.
6 Thompson, D. & Rubenstein, R. 2000. Learning mathematics vocabulary: Potential pitfalls and instructional strategies. *The Mathematics Teacher*, 93/7, pp. 568–574.
7 https://www.theconfidentteacher.com/2022/01/commonly-confused-academic-vocabulary/
8 Quigley, A. 2018. *Closing the vocabulary gap.* Abingdon: Routledge.

6 Words in combination and context

Alice Deignan

Introduction

So far in this book, we have written about words individually, as if they were produced completely separately from each other. Of course, this is not the case. In fact, words come together to make up coherent texts. In this chapter, we look how children might struggle with words in the combinations and contexts of disciplinary registers, and how we can support them with this.

Collocation: words in combination

Defining collocation

Think about any experience you have of learning a foreign language. You may have used a paper or online dictionary to find the words that express what you want to say, but by itself, doing this would not lead to natural sounding sentences. The Macmillan English Dictionary website says 'we do not construct sentences out of single and separate words... words are rarely used as separate pieces of language. They work together in predictable combinations'.[1] The website gives the example of *crazy*, and explains that it is used in combinations like 'be crazy to do something', 'crazy about somebody', 'crazy about something', 'drive somebody crazy', 'go crazy', 'like crazy'. Ron Carter wrote that in theory, any word might be found near any other word, but in reality this does not happen.[2] Words hang out with their regular mates. Collocation is everywhere, in every sentence.

In languages that we speak fluently, we have learned collocations through the many, many times we have heard them. Most word combinations are so well known to us in our everyday language that we would never normally think about them, and we would certainly not think that they are difficult.

We may notice young children making mistakes with collocation. I heard a child aged about two say (with great excitement) 'Look! Dat car poorly!', when he saw

DOI: 10.4324/9781032645513-7

Box 6.1   Collocation

Within linguistics, the term 'collocation' is used to describe how a particular word often tends to be used in combination with other specific words. Some examples:

■ The word *bark* is often (but not always) found in the same sentence as the word *dog*, in sentences like 'she rang the bell and the dog barked'. Linguists would say that *bark* 'collocates' with *dog*.

■ We usually talk about *heavy rain*, not *strong* or *hard rain*, so we would say that *heavy* 'collocates with' *rain*.

■ The phrase 'bringing in money for charity' sounds a bit odd because the usual collocation is '*raising* money for charity'.

---

a car that had been badly damaged in a road traffic accident. He was generalising from having heard *poorly* used to describe people who were unwell. Of course, this sounds odd because although the meaning is more or less right, *poorly* does not usually collocate with words for inanimate objects, only people, and perhaps animals. The child would have learned quickly that the more usual word for a car would be *wrecked* or similar.

Collocations in different registers

Even for adults, collocations are not easy at all if we are speaking a language we don't know well, or if we are speaking a register of our language that we are not very familiar with. Here is a sentence from a law report, a register that I know almost nothing about.

He submits that it follows from the authorities, such as Behbehani v Salem [1989] that where, on his application without notice for a freezing injunction, the claimant has been guilty of deliberate non-disclosure or misrepresentation of facts which (if known) would have defeated his application, the court is precluded from continuing or re-granting a freezing injunction and that this is so even if the claimant files additional evidence on the defendant's application to discharge the injunction....

This extract contains two uses of the word *freezing*, which has a specialist meaning in law that is distantly related to the everyday meaning of 'so cold that water is turning to ice'. (This is an example of the polysemy that we discussed in the previous chapter, where a specialist register uses words with different meanings from their everyday ones.) In the register of law reports, the words that follow *freezing* most often are *order/ orders* and *injunction/ injunctions*. The verb that usually comes before *freezing orders* is usually *discharge,* in a sentence like:

No further application was made to *discharge the freezing orders* prior to the conclusion of the trial.

These collocations are specialised to the register of law reports. Other collocations from this register that people do not use in everyday language are *defeated his application* and *court is precluded from*. As a non-expert, I would not have been able to predict any of these collocations, and I am not completely sure I really understand them. I would need much more experience of reading this register before I'd be able to produce specialist collocations correctly.

My experience of trying to understand this piece of text might be similar to a Year 7 student using a Key Stage 3 worksheet. As well as having new meanings, words now seem to combine in ways that the student has not seen before, and they might not be confident at all that they can produce these collocations correctly in their own writing. In the following sentences, taken from resources designed for KS3 Science, there are some collocations that are discipline-specific, and less usual in everyday language. We have underlined the words that we are focusing on.

1. This is the energy that all the chemical reactions in the body require each day because this amount replaces the energy transferred from their chemical <u>store</u> that day.

2. Scientists are trying to help prevent these species from becoming extinct, and therefore maintain biodiversity. One way is by using gene <u>banks</u>. Gene banks store genetic samples from different species.

3. Glucose and oxygen are <u>carried</u> round your body in the blood.

4. The blood then <u>transports</u> the carbon dioxide to the lungs where you breathe it out.

Think for a minute about what the usual collocates, in everyday language, might be of *store*, *bank*, *carried* and *transports*.

We used our computer corpus of everyday language, the British National Corpus, which we've used previously in this book, to search for the usual collocates of these words and found:

Store: the words that are usually used before (to the left of) *store* are *department*, *chain*, *furniture* and *grocery*. The phrase *chemical store* does occur twice in the BNC, but in both examples, it means 'building where chemicals are stored'.

Bank: the words that are usually used to the left are the names of commercial banks, such as *Barclays*, types of bank, such as *central* and *savings*, and words related to the other meaning, *river*. In everyday language, a collocation like *gene bank* would be very rare.

Carried: the top collocates describing things that are carried in the BNC are *passengers, trays, guns, drinks, luggage, banners, bags, a cup, coffee, a glass*. These are very concrete, tangible, everyday objects, unlike *glucose* and *oxygen*.

Transports: (when used as a verb, like in the Science resource above). The top collocates describing things that are transported are *passengers, freight, coal, cargo, containers, supplies, materials, barrels, oil, grain*. These evoke large scale road and rail transport.

This absolutely does not mean that there is anything wrong with the sentences in the resources. As we have mentioned previously, we are not recommending changing the texts that are currently used. Students need to learn disciplinary registers as part of their developing curriculum expertise. We are looking at details of words in order to be more aware of the challenges that they might present to our students.

Collocation and reading

The linguist Michael Hoey[3] is one of a number of experts who claim that collocation is psychological, that is, we store collocations together in our brains. It makes sense: when we speak, we produce at least two words a second, sometimes more, and normally our listeners can follow at this speed. A fluent adult reader can read at up to four words per second. If we were producing speech by choosing one word at a time, or, as a listener or reader, if we were decoding one word at a time, these speeds would be impossible. We can only speak and understand as quickly as we do because a lot of words are stored in small groups of two, three or more word clusters or chunks, and mostly fished out in these ready-made groups. Sometimes this is called 'pre-fabricated language'.[4]

There is some evidence that children learn parts of their first language in chunks: phrases like 'It's all right', 'let me', 'I'm going to' and 'you have to' may be learned as single units. For some children, it is only when they learn to read and write that they see these phrases as sequences of separate words.

Hoey writes that when we read or hear a word, the words that usually collocate with it are 'primed', that is, we get ready to recognise the words that we are used to seeing or hearing with it. He writes 'a listener, previously given the word *body*, will recognise the word *heart* more quickly than if they had previously been given an unrelated word such as *trick*; in this sense, *body* primes the listener for *heart*' (p. 8).

According to Hoey, we develop 'primings' of words through our repeated encounters with them in language. Taking the word *freezing* for example, which I discussed above in the legal text. As an English-speaking adult, I will have heard this word many thousands of times. The British National Corpus shows that its typical collocates are *fog, temperatures, cold, icy, snow, weather, water, wind, point* and *winter*. If the BNC is similar to the kinds of language that I meet day to day, then these words will be primed when I read or hear *freezing*. When I read *freezing injunction*, *injunction* has not been primed for me by *freezing*, because I do not have experience of reading this legal report register. I can understand it (just about, and not perfectly) but it will slow me down. A Year 7 student might be in a similar position when they read that 'The blood then transports carbon dioxide to the lungs'. *Transports* will prime *passengers*, *cargo* and similar words for them, but not *carbon dioxide*, so their reading will be slowed down.

Different subjects, different collocates

In the examples I showed above, the same word has different collocates in everyday language from a specialist register. Sometimes there are different collocates across subjects, which is not surprising given that we saw that the same word can have different meanings in different subjects. For example, for *independent*, the top three collocates for KS3 Science and History are shown in Table 6.1. (The software has calculated words up to five places before and five places after. I have only shown the top three because beyond that the numbers are too low to make a robust statistical calculation.)

Table 6.2 shows the collocates for *tension* in Science and English.

Table 6.1 Top collocates of *independent* in KS3 Science and KS3 History

Science	
Variable	When drawing results table, the *independent variable* goes in the left hand column.
Dependent	If both your *dependent* and *independent* variables are continuous, then you should plot a line graph.
Categoric	Is the *independent variable categoric* or continuous?
History	
Become	In 1962, the French withdrew and Algeria *became independent*.
Nation	They should become *independent nations*.
State	... Free and *independent states*.

Table 6.2 Top collocates of *tension* in KS3 Science and KS3 English

Science	
Compression	Label parts of an object in *tension* or *compression*.
Stretched	What force did the springs have when you *stretched* them? Tension.
Force	This *force* is called *tension*.
English	
Build	[The author] cleverly uses short sentences to *build* up *tension*.
Suspense	... Does this add to *tension* and *suspense*?
Create	*Tension* is *created* in 'The Battle' through descriptions of Grendel...

Two or three words, but just one idea

So far I've written about how words with separate meanings find themselves hanging out together more often than random probability would predict. As Ron Carter put it 'we might expect *snow* to have a high probability of co-occurrence with *block, road, fall, winter, cold* etc but a low probability of co-occurrence with *cider, apple, dog* etc'.[5] Although the words go together, they seem to keep their individual identities in these examples.

There is a second way in which collocations might slow students down, or cause problems in understanding. Collocations of two or three words sometimes describe a single idea or thing. For example, in British English, the word *school* is most often used after the words *primary* or *secondary*, describing, obviously, primary schools and secondary schools. It is most often used before the words *curriculum, library, leavers, teachers* and *meals,* again each describing a single idea or thing. These are very straightforward ideas, especially to education professionals in the UK. However, to somebody from a different language or culture, some of these collocations, like *school leavers* and *(free) school meals* might not be obvious. A *school leaver* is not a pupil leaving school at the end of the day, but a young adult who has finished their school days and is moving on to the next stage of life. *School meals* are not provided in every country, and the system of free school meals for some children is not straightforward to understand for an outsider.

Moving onto disciplinary registers, collocations of two or three words can describe ideas that are not straightforward and that need specialist knowledge to understand. In Key Stage 3 Maths, the words that are most often used before *factor* are *scale, prime* and *(highest) common.* The expressions *scale factor, prime factor* and *highest common factor* have very specialised meanings, which cannot necessarily be understood by knowing the meaning of the individual words. *Highest* and *common* are words that virtually all Year 7 students would know, but this does not guarantee them understanding their meaning in the collocation *highest common factor.* The phrase has a single meaning. Once we know it, we can see how it is derived from the three words *highest, common* and *factor,* but it would be difficult to work out the meaning from the separate words without help.

In Key Stage 3 Science, one of the words most often used to after *energy* is *store,* making the collocation *energy store,* which has a technical meaning. As we saw above, in everyday English, a *store* is normally where we keep things that are concrete and easily visualised, and quite often describes a shop that sells these things.

Collocation: what are the implications for students?

I've shown that every written and spoken text is full of collocations, that is, conventional ways of putting certain words together. Because we know thousands of these collocations subconsciously, we can produce chunks of words together when we write and speak. When we are listening or reading, our knowledge of collocation helps us to predict what is coming next. All of this helps us to speak and write, read and listen far more quickly than we could if we had to process each individual word separately. However, if we are confronted with a register that we don't know, it's not always obvious which words should go together in writing and speaking. If a text has collocations that are not familiar to us, we're likely to struggle to read it at normal speed because we can't use the usual strategy of predicting what is coming. Sometimes two apparently easy words go together to make a collocation that is not easy to understand, and not easy to work out from the meanings of the individual words.

We think that this shows the importance of using extended phrases or full sentences with students, rather than presenting words in isolation. Knowing what a word means can only take us so far; to be able to read at speed and use it effectively, we need to be able to see how words interact with other words in their disciplinary register. We recommend the use of multiple examples where possible. In previous chapters, we recommended online dictionaries,[6] which have examples that have been retrieved from corpora by skilled lexicographers. The British National Corpus can be searched over the internet[7] for examples from everyday language.

Using the wider language context for meaning

The chapter so far has looked at words in their context, and stressed the importance of context. In this section, I turn this round, and look at what context tells us about meaning. I'm going to argue that it doesn't tell us as much as we think it might. It is not unusual to ask students to work out the meaning of an unknown word from its context. In reality, I think that this is not easy at all, because language is very economical – we don't usually say the same thing more than once in a sentence, so there are not many clear clues to the meaning of a word from the other words around it.

Here are some examples of students in Year 7 trying to work out the meaning of words from context. The examples come from the interviews we described in Chapter 1. They are each with different groups of students, from different schools, and there were many more extracts like this in our interview data where students struggled to work out meaning.

Interview extract 6.1   Students trying to work out the meaning of *fertile*

Students had read: 'Granada's fertile valley and sweeping hills...'

Researcher: there is a word Granada's fertile valley what is fertile?
Aris: fertile is like is it like a range of like things it's like like there's a range of different things and it's kind of
Researcher: so could you infer the meaning of fertile here?
Aris: it's like so let's say there was like a restaurant like an Italian restaurant and then there was like a Chinese restaurant and different kinds it would kinda be like fertile 'cos like there's like different things there and it's not all like the same and it's like different like cultures and stuff.

Interview extract 6.2   Students trying to work out the meaning of
culture

Students had read: 'check out Granada's edgier barrio culture'.

Researcher: what is culture then? what is culture?
Eva: is it like a model?
Zach: ooh culture that's land
Eva: as in? I don't know
Researcher: you don't know
Lily: what?
Niall: land innit? culture
Researcher: culture
Eleanor: is it isn't it like a religion or something... it's like a thing that like
they do like

Interview extract 6.3   Students trying to work out the meaning of
established

Students had read: 'There was a sharp increase in the number of people leaving Walsham. From poor labouring folk with little to give up, to long established families selling their land and stock in return for ready cash'.

Researcher: ... and what about established then?
Chloe: I think it might mean like like a like wealthy?
Researcher: wealthy mhm
Chloe: something like that

We can see that students are coming up with quite plausible suggestions for what the unknown words mean. In 6.1, Aris thinks that a *fertile* valley would be one in which a wide range of different crops grow. This would make sense in the context. In 6.2, Zach seems to be using his knowledge of the word *agriculture* to infer that *culture* means 'land', and this is a definition that might, just, fit with the context. Eleanor is getting closer to the meaning with her suggestion that it is something to do with religion, things people do. In 6.3, it is easy to see why Chloe thinks that *established* might mean 'wealthy', as it is explicitly contrasted with *poor* in the reading text. When we know ourselves what a word means, inferring it from context seems straightforward, but it is often not as helpful as we think.

While it can be difficult to work out a word meaning from a single example, again, multiple examples can help. Going back to the legal register that I quoted from earlier, here is an example of a word that was unknown to me before writing this chapter, *comparator*:

'the addition of a new *comparator* to an equal pay claim represents a new course of action' (from a report of an employment tribunal, in a corpus of legal reports)

I tried to use my knowledge of the verb *compare*, but this didn't help very much. When I looked at another three examples though, I started to get a better sense of meaning.

An appropriate *comparator* would be another counsellor.

The tribunal consider that an appropriate *comparator* in this case was a hypothetical younger, white female who was accused of the same breaches of discipline as the claimant.

[could she] properly compare herself with a male *comparator* doing like work and paid at a higher rate?

This helped me to get to the Merriam Webster[8] definition 'a device for comparing something with a similar thing or a standard measure', and the use specific to legal tribunals, a real or hypothetical example of another individual who has different characteristics, as a test for whether there has been discrimination. With hindsight, the meaning seems obvious but before looking at more examples, then checking dictionaries, it was not. We suggest then that where possible, students are shown several examples, not just one, with plenty of context. Given what we know about polysemy from the previous chapter, dictionary definitions should be checked carefully with them as well.

Conclusion

This chapter has moved on from individual words to look at how words are used in continuous text. This book has presented a lot of lists of words, but the argument we are making now is that words belong with other words, and we can't properly understand them in isolation. In order to be successful at speaking, listening, reading and writing, perhaps especially reading, our students need to have secure networks of words, not just decontextualised lists of meanings.

In the next two chapters, we move on to how our findings about words can be used to support students at this phase of their schooling.

Notes

1 https://macmillandictionaries.com/MED-Magazine/January2009/52-LA-LexicalPriming.htm

2 Carter, R. 2012. *Vocabulary: Applied linguistic perspectives*. Taylor and Francis.

3 Hoey, M. 2005. *Lexical priming: A new theory of words and language*. Routledge.

4 Wray, A. 2000. Formulaic sequences in second language teaching: Principle and practice. *Applied Linguistics*, 21/4, pp. 463–489.

5 Carter, R. 2012. *Vocabulary: Applied linguistic perspectives*. Taylor and Francis, p. 63.

6 https://www.oxfordlearnersdictionaries.com/; https://www.ldoceonline.com/; https://dictionary.cambridge.org/

7 http://www.natcorp.ox.ac.uk/

8 https://www.merriam-webster.com/

7 Selecting and teaching

Marcus Jones

Introduction

Look at those timetables; Table 7.1 gives a typical one. That's a lot of lessons, a lot of learning, and of course a lot of words. It is worth repeating one of the statistics from the project to emphasise the point: more than 2000 new word types over the course of Science in Years 7 and 8. If we assume three Science lessons a week for 39 weeks across two years that gives 234 Science lessons. That means, on average, around eight or nine new words per lesson. Of course, other subjects during the day may have fewer novel words, but even if that is the case, those hours are not oases of time for newly learned words to bed down into adolescent brains.

Table 7.1 A weekly timetable for a Year 7 student at one of the project schools

	Monday	**Tuesday**	**Wednesday**	**Thursday**	**Friday**
Period 1	Geography	Computing	Religion, Philosophy and Ethics	Maths	Science
Period 2	Physical Education	Art	History	Geography	Physical Education
Period 3	PSHE	French	Maths	Science	Drama
Period 4	French	Science	Food and Textiles	English	Music
Period 5	Design Technology	English	English	History	Maths

DOI: 10.4324/9781032645513-8

Instead, pupils' focus will, quite understandably, be taken in entirely new curriculum directions, drawing cognitive attention away from that newly learned and therefore very vulnerable Science information.

When you start to crunch some of the numbers around word volume it can start to feel rather overwhelming. It feels reminiscent of a television advert from over 20 years ago when Budweiser became the official beer sponsors of Premier League football in the UK. They released an amusing advert sharing their 'vision' for football which gently mocked the differences between US and UK sporting expectations – Monster Trucks as half-time entertainment was one such suggestion. It was all very tongue in cheek, but certainly a notch or so above the normal run of the mill half-time adverts.

The moment from that advert that feels most pertinent to word volume is Budweiser's suggestion that they will do away with draws and instead have extra time multi-ball to decide the winner. The advertising hoardings drop down and scores of extra footballs are launched onto the pitch. Players look around confused, some are unwittingly struck by the new rotund arrivals and the advert cuts away, leaving you safe in the knowledge that chaos and confusion will reign.

It feels like the sheer quantity of words pupils experience in the classroom at any phase is akin to those multiple new balls being launched onto the pitch. Added to that complexity is the different mediums through which the words are unleashed. Language comes at pupils from many sources during a lesson: Powerpoint slides; written onto smart or whiteboards; worksheets; text books; and of course many of these overlaid with teacher talk. Little wonder then that pupils may feel like that unsuspecting player hit on the back of the head by a ball they never saw coming.

Of course, our classrooms cannot become like a football pitch where there is only one ball to focus on. Words are the necessary medium of our lessons and so there will always be scores of them flying around every hour. However, this is where selection of those words becomes a vital process that will underpin a pupils' ability to navigate a lesson – indeed a series of lessons – and not feel they have been clonked on the head several times by the sheer weight of words. It is so important, at any phase of teaching, that we do not underestimate the sheer difficulty for pupils grappling with unfamiliar language.

Picking the right words

Consider one topic you are teaching this year. It might span a few weeks, half-a-term, perhaps it even stretches for longer. Now give yourself 2 minutes and write down a list of the key words you think learners require for this topic.

Done that?

I find it is a task that is both pleasing – because you realise the sheer range of interesting things you will cover – but also jolting because you realise the *sheer range* of interesting things you will cover.

A key first principle in selection is that realisation of how many words and how much content you will cover. And while it will all feel absolutely essential, there are decisions to be made about where to put your emphasis. If we launch all those words at pupils in a scattergun approach, some words will stick, others will not. Plus knowing which words will stick becomes more random.

Depth, connectivity, longevity

The process of selection is of course a tricky and inevitably imperfect balancing act and consideration must be given to depth, connectivity and longevity, as covered in Table 7.2.

Conducting the task suggested at the beginning of this section as an individual teacher, or perhaps group of teachers, can be a useful starting point. But from that first list it is likely you will need to streamline your choices. It is important to say that the words you remove are not being removed from the curriculum. Of course they will still feature in lessons, on knowledge organisers and handouts, and will be spoken about in class. However, in that tricky balancing act you are deciding that other words will be amplified more, remembering that doing that successfully with your chosen words will increase the likelihood of the words you cut from 'the list' being learned.

This process of working from a longlist towards a shortlist is a useful and fascinating one as it requires you to really start considering the cornerstones of your curriculum. Which words really house the vital knowledge you want pupils to know? There is, of course, a danger of reductionism here: if you narrow down too much, suddenly years' worth of curriculum might become just three key words.

Table 7.2 Depth, connectivity, longevity

Depth	Select words that require some unpicking and explanation. Words that pupils may pick up more implicitly, or that may not be crucial to the learning will be less valuable. The lesson time you have available should be sensibly weighed against how many words you select. For example, a Key Stage 3 Music teacher with one hour a week understandably wants to balance time taken to explicitly teach key musical vocabulary with the desire for pupils to listen to and create music.
Connectivity	Select words that may connect to: a. other ideas within that topic b. other topics that year c. other subject areas if appropriate.
Longevity	Select words that will support pupils across not just one but multiple lessons and into future years of study.

Table 7.3 KS2 and KS3 examples for depth, connectivity, longevity

	Invasion KS2 History example	Variable KS3 Science example
Depth	Both words require some explanation to truly get at their meaning for the respective contexts	
Connectivity 1. other ideas within that topic 2. other topics that year 3. other subject areas if appropriate	1. Invasion is often an attempt to gain power and leads to a place having new rulers. 2. In the KS2 National Curriculum[1] invasion is mentioned in topics about the Romans, Vikings, Anglo-Saxons and Scots 3. PE invasion games	1. Variables might be dependent or independent in an experiment 2. Introduction to investigations; forces; digestion, nutrition and health 3. Maths, Geography
Longevity future study	The Norman conquest, empires, the Second World War	Required practicals at Key Stage 4 whereby pupils must conduct certain experiments

Again though, it is important to reiterate we are not removing other words from the curriculum, just elevating certain words to enable them to receive that little bit more exposure. I give examples of how Depth, Connectivity and Longevity would apply to word choice for topics in History and Science, in Table 7.3.

In terms of how many words is the right amount, there is no set answer here. How long the topic runs for, how many hours of lesson time you have a week and how much time within a lesson might be required to dig into key words in more detail need to be attended to. The importance of what students know already must be factored in (for more on assessment see Chapter 8). We must also factor in that words taught in one lesson will not be instantly learned and we need to find time to return to and consolidate the understanding of a word. Furthermore, what it takes to 'know' a word is complex and involves many interactions, as described in Chapter 1, so we want to ensure we select words that will be frequently seen and used, becoming an essential part of the taught content.

Disciplinary literacy supports classroom delivery

Shanahan and Shanahan write: 'A disciplinary literacy approach emphasizes the specialised knowledge and abilities possessed by those who create, communicate, and use knowledge within each of the disciplines'.[2]

Have you got a favourite topic? One you have taught many times before and that each year still delights you when it is time deliver it once more? The types of topics where you feel you have that fullness of knowledge, where you can take the learning into really interesting places, in engaging ways, but safe in the knowledge that you can still drive home the core knowledge and skills. You've got disciplinary expertise right there. And bound up in that will be your disciplinary literacy knowledge: how to support successful pupil writing and knowing how best to present certain text that will aid the learning. And from a vocabulary stand point, knowing which are the best words to teach, and how to really get at their essential meaning for that particular topic.

There are understandable instances where we might not feel like the fount of all knowledge in a particular field. Yet even then, we can be confident that our knowledge base still remains at least a few steps ahead of the pupils.

Remembering this feels important when making our word selections. It is empowering for classroom practitioners because they are the holders of what Shanahan and Shanahan refer to as the 'specialised knowledge and abilities'. Put simply: they know the right stuff to teach. It is not feasible, or indeed helpful, for one person – a literacy lead perhaps – to make all central decisions about which words to teach, because they will not have that requisite level of knowledge in different topic areas. So disciplinary literacy places the responsibility for selection with those that do have that knowledge. This feels right. Therefore, the role of a centralised literacy lead, or a teaching and learning coordinator becomes much more about establishing decent principles (such as depth, connectivity, longevity) and then facilitating the requisite time and support for the experts to make their selections.

In primary schools, teachers have the pleasure and benefit of experiencing the word load of their pupils throughout the day. This can help in the selection process when considering the quantity of new words that might be introduced during one day. It also gives a strong base from which to make connections between key words as you know what has come before that day and can draw timely links that might not be explicit on a central word list.

So when making our word selections let's make sure we check with the people that know. The holders of that disciplinary literacy knowledge. They can take a top 10 list from the corpus and begin to tell you which words will work best for the topics they teach. By accessing the expertise provided by teachers who have taught that topic to that phase before, we can ensure our word choices are pertinent and powerful for our pupils.

Making selections in the different subject areas

Corpus top 10s

The thinking outlined in this chapter so far can be applied to practitioners of any phase and subject. Taking time to consider a more coherent vocabulary selection linked to the curriculum is likely to be extremely useful for a range of teachers.

If you are looking specifically at vocabulary at the transition, a useful mechanism to get the selection started involves the findings of the project.

After slicing the corpus to find out how many new words there are for different subject areas and for different key stages, words can then be filtered for frequency. In Tables 7.4 and 7.5 you can see the outcome of this, a cut-down version of the lists in Chapter 4. Words are listed alphabetically, not in absolute rank order of frequency. We have removed words that seemed far more dependent on topic choice e.g. 'castle' in Macbeth. This is in an attempt to give a sense of those words that might provide the broadest use to schools.

Table 7.4 Words more frequent at KS2 than KS3

Maths	Science	English	History	Geography
Identical	Adaptive	Adverbial	Afterlife	Compass
Model	Creature	Clause	Ancient	Dam
Numeral	Evolution	Conjunction	Axis	Delta
Other frequent words are a collection of concrete nouns common to practical examples of maths problems e.g. apple, crayon, jar	Invention	Exclamation	Egyptian	Fairtrade
	Invertebrate	Parenthesis	Goddess	Floodplain
	Mammal	Prefix	Locomotive	Footbridge
	Micro-organism	Root	Pharaoh	Iron (earth's crust)
	Plastic	Subjunctive	Pyramid	Length
	Reptile	Subordinate	Tomb	River
	Vertebrate	Suffix	Viking	Tectonic

Table 7.5 Words more frequent at KS3 than KS2

Maths	Science	English	History	Geography
Angles	Acid	Analyse	Agree	Climate
Corresponding	Atom	Annotate	Change	Development
Decrease	Compound	Create	Contribute	Environment
Enlargement	Element	Discuss	Control	Effect
Factorise	Mass	Effect	Evidence	Location
Multiplier	Particle	Evidence	Relatively	Natural
Probability	Pressure	Explore	Rival	Population
Sample	React	Reader	Revolutionise	Physical
Significant	State	Theme	Significant	Scale
Substitute	Transfer	Writer	Sources	Sparse

The work of Beck et al.[3] on word tiers has been an important boon to teacher understanding about the function of words. Understanding the different tiers (see Chapter 3) can feed into the decision-making process around word selection. Often, the more overt difficulty of tier 3 words may nudge us towards selecting those, but it is crucial to consider words which might be considered tier 2 – perhaps even tier 1 in some instances – and which may actually underpin many key principles of our subject. The importance of these words may possibly surprise us but only because our familiarity with them has maybe rendered them more mundane.

For a KS3 English lesson the novelty of a word like 'oxymoron' may feel appealing to introduce and teach in some detail during a poetry unit, but if it does not pass muster against our principles of longevity, depth and connectivity it may not be the best selection to support students. Whereas, the far more common 'reader' and 'effect' may be more important to create a foundation of understanding for pupils.

Or for a primary History topic on Ancient Greeks, 'polytheism' may indeed feature and be explained, but do we want to amplify and return to it as much as 'civilisation' which will more likely to connect to a wider range of History topics?

When looking for some of these key foundational principles to consider teaching at the transition, the below summaries may be useful for practitioners to digest. Again, it is important to highlight that in instances where we draw a distinction between KS2 and 3, it is not to say none of that aspect is being done at KS2 (or vice versa), rather that the frequency of it is reduced.

Maths – from concrete to abstract

The application of mathematics to everyday situations in KS2 is increasingly replaced by abstract descriptions of a mathematical problem.

> KS2 – Tilly has £20. She gives £5.40 to her friend. Tilly now has twice as much money as her friend. How much money did her friend have at the start?
> KS3 – Two children share £30. Child A has x pounds, Child B has twice as much. How much do they each have?

Possible words to consider: apply, expression, simplify

Science – the challenge of polysemy

Do not assume that everyday knowledge of words will suffice for the disciplinary demands of Science. The distinction here is not that words within science lessons at KS2 utilise the more everyday tier 1 or 2 meanings, while at KS3 it is suddenly all tier 3 usage. Polysemy is present in both, but the frequency of polysemous words increases at KS3. Therefore, selections in science need to be alert to those words with multiple meanings benefitting from more careful exposition.

Possible words to consider: force, cell, speed

English – authorial intention

2023 KS2 English Reading Test,[4] question 37
The first words Innis said to the boy were: 'Where are you going?'
Why did Innis want to know where the boy was going?
Example KS3 English test question
What effect does Owen's presentation of war have on the reader?

The fact that the writer is mentioned more frequently at KS3 than KS2 is perhaps not surprising when the KS3 National Curriculum for English mentions 'knowing the purpose, audience for and context of the writing and drawing on this knowledge to support comprehension'.[5]

This phrase does not feature at KS2 and marks a shift towards seeing a text as the result of a writer-reader interaction. Consequently, word selections across the transition may look to build the body of knowledge that helps pupils to understand this key relationship.

Possible words to consider: writer, create, reader, effect

History – the reasons for and nature of change

In a not dissimilar shift to that seen in English, there begins to be a greater focus on the reasons for something. Instead of considering an author, it becomes about a consideration of reasons for events and the speed and significance of changes as a result.

Possible words to consider: change, contribute, relatively, significant

Geography – time changes everything

There is a shift away from naming and descriptions of physical spaces and places, to bigger concepts of geography and the processes involved.

Possible words to consider: climate, scale, physical

Summary points on selection

The utterly essential work of selecting vocabulary for explicit instruction should not be underestimated. Earlier in this chapter we established three key principles to guide this:

- Depth

- Connectivity

- Longevity

We offer the project corpus subject lists as a useful tool to aid selection, but know its true benefit is likely to be felt when used in tandem with existing schemes of learning and practitioner expertise from both KS2 and 3.

Approaches to teaching vocabulary

'When children 'know' a word, they not only know the word's definition and its logical relationship with other words, they also know how the word functions in different contexts'.

Stahl, S. A., & Kapinus, B. (2001)[6]

In earlier chapters we have spoken about the idea of words as artefacts. But artefacts come in many different guises: stumble across a gold coin or a buried jewel and your interest is likely to be immediately piqued. In the same way, both teachers and pupils may find more interest in new and novel vocabulary they encounter, and on many occasions these will be the type of words Beck categorised as tier 3.

In contrast, encountering a half-buried wooden plate might feel familiar to the extent of disinterest, in the same way that words such as 'reader', 'evidence' and 'energy' may make pupils (and teachers) assume knowledge is secure because of their familiarity with the word. Or we might even assume that half-knowledge of these words is sufficient to get by in the lesson. As the project data has shown, many of the frequently used words in subjects at both key stages are not highly complex, polysyllabic words, but are words pupils will have seen and heard before and may automatically feel they have a good understanding of. Herein lies danger though, as we have seen from pupil interviews [Chapter 1] that familiarity with a word in one context does not lead to instant understanding of that same word in a different context.

It seems important then that we have methods in our classroom that allow the specific meaning of a word to begin to be unpacked. By spending time highlighting the different uses of a word in different contexts we shine light on our artefact and make what was an old wooden bowl/'word I already know', be seen in a new light.

The analogy (perhaps already stretched too thin!) begins to diverge at the next stage because whereas it is, we assume, frowned upon for ancient artefacts to be picked up and handled, what we very much want to create in the classroom is the opportunity to pick up and handle the words. A fair amount of mishandling might be expected at this stage as pupils get to grips with the words, try using it themselves and deepen their understanding of the vocabulary. We do not want words to just be encased in laminated word lists on the wall, instead we want those words to be out of the box being used and utilised to their full extent.

Features of effective vocabulary instruction

- Define the word
- Know the word
- Record the knowledge
- Check understanding

Define the word

Trade: the activity of buying and selling, or exchanging, goods and/or services between people or countries[7]

Just copying and pasting a dictionary definition can be problematic. Firstly, as the definition above shows, there might be some equally problematic language in the definition: goods and services would need a bit of explaining I suspect.

Secondly, as the sections on polysemy and disciplinary literacy have indicated, it is important that pupils are given a clear definition of the word related to the subject area and context they will require it for. In doing this, teachers may also contrast the required definition against other uses and definitions of the words. Making these differences explicit is all part of building a rounded understanding of the word.

We want our definitions to feel usable, repeatable (overlong definitions are to be avoided) and relevant to the topic area. So, returning to the word 'trade': how about 'buying and selling'.

Know the word

To help pupils know the word better, activities and tasks that help pupils use and play with the word are important. There are a huge range of options available and deciding which one to use will include thinking about existing practice, available resources and the requirements of different subjects. The list below gives some ideas:

Hearing the word

How would you pronounce the following word: sesquipedalian. Even if you know the word (it means to use a lot of long words), the chances are you will not have used it much recently and needing to say it out loud would have felt a little rusty. It could be assisted by a phonetic spelling (sess-kwih-pid-ay-lee-in) which is something you might consider including in methods to unpack words. Equally, modelling the correct pronunciation to pupils a phoneme at a time (while clapping the syllables) and providing the opportunity to practise and repeat will help the word lodge in the brain. If you cannot hear the word correctly in your inner voice you will be far less likely to remember and use the word again.

Frayer model

The Frayer model presents a four box grid with the key word at the centre. The traditional headings, as developed by Dorothy Frayer at the University of Wisconsin in the 1960s, are: definition; characteristics (features) of the word; examples; non-examples. Alterations to those original headings are not uncommon, with synonyms, antonyms, etymology and images often being incorporated as befits the need. It might also be interesting to consider where collocates (Chapter 6) could be included in such a grid to build knowledge of which other words pupils are likely to encounter alongside the featured word (Table 7.6).

Table 7.6 Frayer model for climate

Definition	Characteristics
The average weather over at least 30 years.	Precipitation
	Temperature
	Climate
Examples	**Non-examples**
The climate of a desert is hot and dry.	Weather: because it is just hour by hour
The climate of the United Kingdom is mild and wet.	rather than a long term average.

Word maps

Building a web of related words, concepts and topics to create a strong sense of how a key word does not exist in isolation, but is interconnected with other knowledge both within and outside the topic in question. Again, factoring in the relationship between the word and its common collocates seems a beneficial addition to such word maps (Figure 7.1).

Morphology and etymology

Understanding the stories and patterns behind words is an incredibly useful tool not only to deepen understanding of an individual word, but to cope with unfamiliar words. Morphology looks at how words can often be broken into roots, prefixes and suffixes and how their constituent meanings can piece together the whole. This is often well allied with etymology which explains the history of the words, providing us with origin tales for our vocabulary.

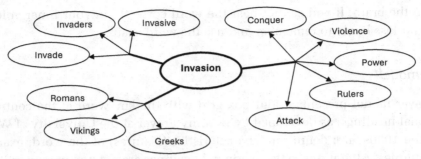

Figure 7.1 Invasion word map for KS2 history.

Pictures and images

A visual prompt can be a powerful way of strengthening the hold the brain has over the word. Pictures can help make more abstract ideas concrete, perhaps bringing them in to real world contexts, while images or symbols can also provide tools for recall and recollection.

Space to talk

Box 7.1   Case study: Wise Academies

Wise Academies is a trust of 13 primary schools in the North East.

Vocabulary work in our schools focuses on the importance of discussion, and for pupils to have the chance to play with language (Table 7.7). This is guided by the 5 Ds: While there is no expectation that all 5 Ds are used every time a word is introduced, it provides a framework for pupils to talk with and around the word.

Centrally designed knowledge organisers provide staff with the core language for topics. These fall into two categories: golden thread words that will occur across more than one topic (these are also displayed in classrooms) and high utility words for that particular topic. Also provided centrally are a bank of retrieval tasks that can be utilised at the start of lessons to prompt recall. Retrieval tasks are also used at the end of each unit to check for understanding.

Stella Jones, Director of Research and Development, Wise Academies

Table 7.7 The 5 Ds

	Description	**Example: Capture**
Define	Teacher provides definition and explains morphology and etymology of the word. Pupils discuss their understanding of what it means and agree on their own wording for a definition. Possible extra: List synonyms	Capture means to take possession of something or someone, usually by force. CAPT is from the Latin 'capare' which means to take/hold/seize.

(Continued)

Table 7.7 (Continued)

	Description	Example: Capture
Divulge	Pairs think of a sentence to showcase how to use the word.	The Romans were masters of the art of siege warfare, allowing them to capture even the strongest of fortresses.
Dictate	Rehearse the sentence orally and then write it down.	The Romans were masters of the art of siege warfare, allowing them to capture even the strongest of fortresses.
Doodle	Pupils may draw a picture to help aid memorisation of the definition.	Pupils create own image.
Dramatise	Pupils act out the word (especially good for verbs).	Pupils might capture a classmate or a peer's possession.

Record knowledge

Pupils will forget words between lessons so having a mechanism to record their knowledge and return to it feels useful. Pupils' exercise books, physical vocabulary booklets or electronic ways of recording can all play a part here and choices may boil down to existing systems within the school and the logistics of what works in the classroom – if the school tablets are unreliable then the electronic record may not be the best fit.

Check understanding

Teaching a word for 10 minutes does not mean it has been learned. Returning to it as a starter in the following lesson will not guarantee it has stuck with all the pupils. We need methods for checking what pupils know about the words. Again, schools may well have existing methods for low stakes checking of pupil knowledge but here is a list of ideas if useful:

● Blank Frayer models

● Multiple Choice Quizzes

● Pupils write the definition

● Spotting whether the word has been used correctly or incorrectly in sentences

● Pupils write their own sentence using the word correctly

- Providing the word and asking pupils to list possible collocates

- Pupils RAG rate their knowledge of the word (perhaps a definition or correct application of the word being required to confirm a 'Green')

From receptive to expressive vocabulary

Box 7.2   Case study: Unity Schools Partnership

Unity Schools Partnership is a trust of 34 primary, secondary and special schools across Suffolk, Essex and Norfolk.

We began our work in earnest in 2018 as it became clear that limited vocabulary was impeding many of our pupils. A team derived from Unity Research School and CUSP (Curriculum with Unity Schools Partnership) began to build the curriculum across years one to nine in History, Geography, Science and English and part of this building included the selection of key vocabulary. These words are listed at the start of each learning module.

The explicit instruction of vocabulary in lessons is built around five steps, derived from the research of Cain and Oakhill (2015)[8] and with the intent to move beyond a definition.

1. **See/hear the word** (opportunities here for I say, you say). KS1 science example – *common*

2. **Define** (opportunities to explore the origins of words). Com – together; mon – go, move

3. **Connect** (activate prior learning). Perhaps an image of two people, with the question: what do they have in common?

4. **Use** (in a sentence, in the context of the lesson). Nitrogen is the most common element in air.

4. **Analyse.** How is the word 'common' functioning in the sentence? What information is it giving us about the make-up of the air?

These steps are crucial to the explicit teaching of the chosen words, but their strength means they can be used when unfamiliar or unplanned for words emerge during teaching.

Following these steps helps pupils to deepen their understanding of the word and build their semantic memory of it. However, we knew that by itself that would not be enough to secure long term expressive vocabulary, so built into the curriculum are scaffolded opportunities for pupils to attempt using the word themselves, followed by independent application tasks. These application tasks sit alongside vocabulary quizzes planned into learning modules to assess pupil understanding.

Lauren Meadows, Curriculum Development Advisor, Unity Schools Partnership

Share forwards

Teachers are familiar with the process of reacting to pupil assessments and using what is known and not known to inform future planning. This takes on an added meaning around the transition as schools will want to consider how information is shared between KS2 and KS3 colleagues in terms of what has been taught, what word knowledge seems to have been learned, and where gaps may still occur [see Chapter 8 for ideas on implementation].

There is no definitive sense in research that any one of the above methods for teaching vocabulary supersedes the others in terms of usefulness. They can all serve a purpose. Indeed, practitioners reading this book may already have different tools they use and as long as they include elements of the Define, Know, Record, Check criteria then those tools will have just as much value.

Beyond the word lists – building a vocabulary culture

'Ambulance' and 'amble' have a common etymology: the Latin 'ambulantem' meaning to walk or go about. While it might feel a strange origin for the former word (a walking speed ambulance does not seem like great news to me), it links to hospitals that were used to support the army. These were constructed in a way that they could be quickly taken to pieces and moved (walked) to the next place it was needed.

Words are interesting and powerful things aren't they? They are little nuggets of knowledge and accruing more of them builds wondrous understanding. And because you can isolate them it is certainly possible to build a coherent strategy for their instruction in the classroom – both in terms of the transition, but also more generally within the classroom at any phase. However, an approach to vocabulary that stops at this can be in danger of limiting the full range of opportunities to embrace new language and all the new learning it represents.

Thinking aloud

Be the model word detective for your pupils. Endeavour to show them your own thinking as you introduce and encounter vital vocabulary. Accompanying any language instruction with a live commentary can provide crucial insight to an expert's thought process as they tackle new language. This can be done whether you have chosen to introduce the word by itself to start with, or whether you plan to encounter it within a wider text. The aim is twofold: to demonstrate curiosity in language – that words are there to be engaged with, not to run from. And secondly, to add more tools to pupil toolboxes for when they encounter new words. They can know the type of questions to ask themselves about vocabulary. As a starting point, we provide some possible prompts and questions practitioners could use for their 'out loud' modelling:

- *How do I say this word? Can I sound it out?*

- *Are there parts of that word that I do recognise?*

- *That's a strange word, I'm going to come back to it.*

- *I have not understood that sentence, perhaps I need to read it again.*

- *Is there anything else in the text that might help me? I know sometimes there is a glossary.*

- *Are there other clues from the sentence that might help me with that word?*

- *Are there words that seem to often be nearby the word I am trying to understand?*

'What does it mean?' – harnessing the curiosity

Pupils love to tussle and grapple with words. In the pupil interviews it was striking how willing they were to think about and generally try to understand the words they were faced with. Teachers and parents will all recognise this curiosity and interest in words from their own children or pupils they have taught. Wanting to know what something means helps build your understanding of the world from a young age. Teachers and parents alike will no doubt recognise those moments following an inquisitive question when you realise you are not entirely sure of the answer yourself! Of course, we can guard against some of this with the steps mentioned earlier in this chapter around selection and unpacking the words, but we can never cover everything and anticipate all the questions that may arise. What remains within our power though is the ability to build a classroom culture that:

- Allows teachers to confidently cope with the implicit moments of instruction and

- Allows pupils to confidently cope with language that is unfamiliar

Much of the ground work for this can be laid in the development of a clear strategy for vocabulary instruction. By building staff knowledge around the selection of key words and building resources around their instruction we equip practitioners and learners with knowledge and strategies for dealing with other words. If we have used morphology and etymology to unpick a selected word then we need to make it clear that this is a tool that can be applied to other vocabulary too. This does not guarantee success of course, because pupils might encounter a word that features no prefix or suffix and is just a root, the origins of which they do not know. However, they are not bereft of other options. The below list offers some potential solutions:

- Emotional regulation: Pupils realising what reaction they might have to tricky words and texts can be a useful starting point. Feeling overwhelmed or wanting to give up are perfectly natural responses and making that acceptable can become a foundation to then build some of the following approaches upon.

- What you already know (text type and words): This is a powerful skill to hone as it demonstrates to pupils that they always bring their existing knowledge to a text. They are never starting from scratch and realising they already know much of value can be a powerful motivation. Allied to this is the merit of orientating yourself within the right discipline. For example, having real clarity that you are reading a science text might allow a pupil to rule out the usefulness of their predominant understanding of 'cell' being something prisoners are kept in.

- Talk: It was noticeable in the pupil interviews how often pupils, with only occasional nudges from the researcher, would engage in detective discussions between themselves to try and figure out what the word meant.

- Re-read for context: While we showed in Chapter 1 that attempting to read in context is not fool proof, it remains an important skill for pupils to develop to prevent them just stopping at the unknown word and not considering its relationship with surrounding words and sentences. This can also be a means of building up knowledge of words and their collocates [Chapter 6].

- Define and move on: In this section we are considering the more implicit moments of vocabulary instruction, not ones that have been specifically planned for. Throwing every tricky word that crops up open to class discussion, or giving time for re-reading will realistically and practically not work in the timeframes of lessons. Sometimes, the best decision will be a quick working definition and then continuing with the text.

Summary points on approaches for teaching vocabulary

How do we get pupils to fully know a word? In Chapter 1, Alice discussed that sense of half-knowing words and phrases like 'hedge fund' and 'quarterly' results. Half-knowing is sometimes enough for the few minutes you spend reading a news article, or indeed for some words that occur within a lessons. It does not feel enough for words so vital to the curriculum that time and care has been spent selecting them. Therefore, to get beyond the half-knowing, it feels important to have strategies for instruction that allow more fulsome understanding of crucial vocabulary. We have suggested principles of:

- Define the word

- Know the word

- Record the knowledge

- Check understanding

Having such a framework can help with the production of resources that can support teachers and pupils. It can also be an important step in developing a culture around vocabulary, building learners' expertise in how to independently handle language that they unearth.

Notes

1 Department for Education (DfE). 2013. The national curriculum in England: History key stages 1 and 2. https://www.gov.uk/national-curriculum
2 Shanahan, C. & Shanahan, T. 2012. What is disciplinary literacy and why does it matter? https://www.shanahanonliteracy.com/publications/what-is-disciplinary-literacy-and-why-does-it-matter
3 Beck, I., McKeown, M. & Kucan, L. 2002. *Bringing words to life: Robust vocabulary instruction.* Guildford Press
4 Material developed by the Standards and Testing Agency for 2023 national curriculum assessments and licensed under Open Government Licence v3.0. https://assets.publishing.service.gov.uk/media/6464d5a0d3231e000c32db4c/2023_key_stage_2_English_reading_answer_booklet.pdf
5 Department for Education (DfE). 2013. *The national curriculum in England: English Key Stage 3.* https://www.gov.uk/national-curriculum
6 Stahl, S. A. & Kapinus, B. 2001. *Word power: What every educator needs to know about teaching vocabulary.* National Education Association.
7 www.dictionary.cambridge.org
8 Oakhill, J., Cain, K. & McCarthy, D. 2015. Inference processing in children: The contributions of depth and breadth of vocabulary knowledge. In O'Brien, E., Cook, A. & Lorch, R. (eds.) *Inferences during reading.* Cambridge University Press, pp. 140–160.

8 Making words work in the classroom

Marcus Jones

Implementation

Effective implementation matters. All attempts at school improvement will give themselves a better chance of success if 'how' the thing is done is given due care and consideration. A vocabulary transition strategy is no different. And while the course of implementation never runs smooth, enhancing an approach to vocabulary remains one of the more manageable areas of literacy practice to address.

Models, frameworks and overarching guides around good implementation, not just within education, all point towards strong principles related to planning, delivering and sustaining an approach, with the vital added elements of time and training.[1]

This chapter seeks to take those principles and begin to apply them more specifically towards aspects of vocabulary at the transition. As has been repeated throughout this book, research looking at vocabulary at the transition is limited so we are not in a position to draw upon large scale projects that have undertaken change in this area. Instead, we want to establish good questions for individuals and schools to ask themselves in the following areas:

- Strategic leadership

- Monitoring and evaluation

- Staff training

- The 5 Ws of word selection

- Resources

Thinking and planning in these areas is likely to take place under different conditions and contexts. While the ideal will almost certainly feature a carefully

DOI: 10.4324/9781032645513-9

co-constructed approach between primary and secondary colleagues, useful change could still be undertaken by an individual school at either phase looking to prepare its pupils better for the step from Year 6 to Year 7.

Strategic leadership

Consider for a moment your most immediate working colleagues. For practitioners in a single form entry primary school, that might be colleagues working with the classes immediately preceding and succeeding your class. For a Maths teacher at a large secondary school, it could be well into double figures, some of whom you can probably go a couple of days without physically seeing if it is the time of year when noses are to the grindstone.

How easy would it be to introduce new practice to that group of colleagues? As a spurious example let's say we are going to ask everyone to start their lessons by singing 'Twinkle, twinkle little star'. Simple enough? But even what seem like simple proposals can flounder because:

● An email was not read (or was misunderstood)

● Someone missed the meeting so was not fully sure on the third line of the song

● Someone else could not sing in their lesson because their throat was hurting

● Someone else did not really see the point of singing 'Twinkle, twinkle, little star' at the start of their lesson

The realities of school life will always put barriers in the way. And when we think of vocabulary at the transition, we are not just trying to harmonise a small group of immediate colleagues. More likely we are looking to get numerous colleagues from different schools to sing from the same song sheet.

It is imperative that strategic leadership is provided. The foundations for this may already be there in roles such as a transition coordinator, or perhaps heads of year. There is further good news in that schools up and down the country already enact numerous supporting mechanisms for transition such as taster days for children and information evenings for parents and carers, so lines of communication and professional relationships are almost certainly well established.

There will still likely be a need to contemplate whether those colleagues remain the best placed to mobilise work related to the curriculum or whether their expertise about the transition as it stands may be usefully supplemented by others with particular curriculum knowledge. Forming a transition leadership group may be useful with representation from different stakeholders to drive forward a transition vocabulary initiative. Such a group is likely to benefit from enough people to enable expertise across the areas shown in Figure 8.1.

Once established, this group has much to deliberate on with the following four section headings maybe forming a useful first agenda.

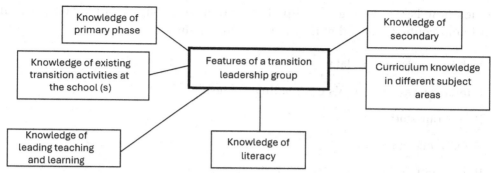

Figure 8.1 Features of a transition leadership group.

Box 8.1   Secondaries with multiple feeder primaries

There are many secondary schools in the country who may require more than both hands and feet to count all their feeder primaries. Here, a transition leadership group as articulated above may not seem quite as feasible. However, while it may not be possible to ensure every feeder primary is represented, there are likely to be primary schools who are better placed to contribute, whether this be because of geographical closeness, or perhaps more likely the number of children they send to the secondary.

The key thing is that there is representation from both phases. It would be a utopian world indeed where the transition leadership group are able to make choices and decisions that factor in the needs of all stakeholder schools. More likely, there will always be some compromises and 'executive decisions' that have to be taken. However, these are given a better chance of success if both primary and secondary colleagues have been consulted in some way.

Finally, the make-up of the group is not set in stone. Colleagues may be added in subsequent years to develop and refine the approach to the academic transition.

Why vocabulary at the transition?

Take a look at your school's development plan, or perhaps your key stage or departmental one: it will be full of important content and useful work to undertake. But as the Education Endowment Foundation states in its original 'Putting Evidence to Work' Guidance Report, 'In our collective haste to do better for pupils, new ideas are often introduced with too little consideration for how the changes will be managed'.[2]

While the vocabulary at the transition project data may speak to some of our anecdotal understanding of the difficulty of making the transition from primary to secondary school, it is essential to consider how this narrative plays out within your own context. Creating time to explore the issue further will be helpful to unpick how issues such as the dip at transition (see Chapter 1) play out in your particular context. Tools that may help do this include:

- In-house assessment data

- Literacy assessment tools e.g. reading age tests

- Behaviour statistics

- Attendance statistics

- Pupil, staff and parent voice about the transition

Several of these may already be used by primaries and secondaries around the transition, so it may not require much tweaking by a transition leadership group to refocus certain questions, or reinterpret data through a more vocabulary focused lens. It is important to say these tools need not all be enacted once Year 7 has started: there is much to be learned in the preceding months.

As ever, the limitations of the data gathered should be considered. For example, if reading age tests are used they will not necessarily drill down into specific issues around vocabulary, so building up a bank of different tools to really get at what the transition issues may be will be beneficial. Equally beneficial will be securing any data gathered in a coherent format. This will help with later monitoring and evaluation.

What does it look like?

The answer to this question will lie in information gleaned from the preceding section – balanced too with an awareness of resources and capacity that are available. But here are some ideas to prompt further discussion:

- A series of summer term sessions for Year 6 pupils to boost knowledge of key terms for Year 7

- A set of dedicated vocabulary sessions in different topic/subject areas across Years 6 and 7 to build vocabulary knowledge

- Building a consistent approach to vocabulary instruction across feeder primaries and associated secondaries

What's the timeframe?

Let's assume that you feel there is work to be done around the academic transition. How does this fit with existing school priorities? You will already be undertaking crucial work in other areas to support pupils and I'm yet to meet a school that feels like it has surplus capacity, so how do we carefully create a timeline to make change in a new area?

Making that timeframe realistic is important, rather than rushing to get something started for the nearest September and assuming in the school calendar it will all be neatly wrapped up by the following July. An added complexity to work at the transition is you will be balancing existing priorities and timelines across different schools. Even in Multi Academy Trusts, or groups of schools used to working together, the chances of all those aspects aligning neatly across schools and phases are slim. This makes the transition leadership group all the more imperative.

One thing seems highly likely: you cannot start too early. We can assume there will be some student facing actions for pupils in the final half-term of Year 6 at the absolute latest. So to give enough time cushion for that, a transition leadership group will find plenty to discuss from as early as Autumn. A key question at this time will be to think about the scale of the approach to begin with: what do we want to do to help pupils with the linguistic transition and which staff will be required as part of this?

What does it mean for staff?

Talk of the transition immediately makes us think about the year groups either side of that line: Years 6 and 7. It is unthinkable that some staff in these year groups won't need to be involved in some capacity in order to make an approach work. Whether it needs to go further than this in the first iterations of a new strategy is an implementation consideration that will need to be balanced against other demands on staff time. Perhaps the approach starts smaller and is introduced to a wider staff body when it has been tested in the cold waters of reality.

Whatever staff may be involved, the vocabulary transition group need to think carefully about ensuring staff buy-in around the importance of the issue. This is both a matter of winning hearts and minds about supporting students, but also includes crucial practical considerations such as giving time to staff to implement a change. What Professional Development time is required (delivered by who?) and does this tally with what PD time is available at the different schools and settings? And how and when do we plan to measure impact?

Box 8.2 Implementation ideas for the individual classroom teacher

Up until this point, our strategic planning has assumed some level of coordination between primaries and a secondary. However, the very suggestion of a transition leadership group will simply not be workable in a whole host of situations. So, what to do if you are reading this as a hardworking classroom teacher in either a primary or secondary classroom who is not in a position to establish some grand cross phase operation. Crucially, the principles still apply.

- Why vocabulary at the transition? What is it that makes you think this is an issue that needs addressing? Is there further evidence you can gather? You might be able to construct your own questionnaire and/or assessment that finds out a little more about what words the pupils know for certain topic or subject areas and this could be the starting point of selecting some words to teach more explicitly.

- What does it look like? Here this becomes a question perhaps of what you want your vocabulary instruction to look like within a lesson and how you build your own consistency in this area [for further ideas see Chapter 7].

- What's the timeframe? This becomes something more of a curriculum question as you consider what vocabulary content you wish to cover and where in the curriculum it fits best.

Monitoring and evaluation

The transition leadership group will want to formulate plans from the outset about what is important to check and measure, and when that should be done. Expecting to do some work on vocabulary at the transition and therefore improve the reading ages of Year 7 pupils will be mightily difficult to prove, so more realistic ways of weighing the value of the work done should be planned for. The idea of weighing value is a useful one here as when undertaking any new initiative in a school we must be open to the possibility that the data we gather may point towards little or no impact and, if weighed against time and workload inputs, decisions may need to be made about the benefits of continuing.

Ideas for what could be measured are included in the Table 8.1, though this is not an exhaustive list.

While Table 8.1 suggests the what and how, it is fundamental to also make decisions about who will collect the data and when. Some of the data gathered and the responses to it may fall within the remit of the leadership group. Other parts, particularly those gathered from the pupils, may need to be shared between staff across phases. For example, if an assessment reveals a lack of understanding around three key words at the end of Year 6, that information will be crucial to share with relevant Year 7 teachers. A timeline showing the what, how, who and when of the monitoring tools will bring clarity to something that may otherwise become easily confused, or perhaps all too often, just forgotten about.

Data gathered will hopefully inform what the approach might look like in the future. If elements of success are seen, what has brought them about? And what areas may need further attention? Either way, if a decision is made to continue we must remember that further roll out or scaling up of an approach will require equal care in its implementation.

Table 8.1 Monitoring and evaluation

What is being gathered?	How is it being gathered?	Further considerations
Pupil knowledge of words	Multiple choice questions Using words correctly in sentences	Can teacher marking load be alleviated by using technology? When should assessments be conducted and how long will they last?
Pupil confidence with words	Scaled response questions	Do you just check confidence around the taught words or see if there is impact on their overall confidence with unfamiliar language?
Pupil application of words in their own work	Written or verbal responses	What is the marking burden? What is the criterion for deciding if the word has been used correctly?
Staff confidence when delivering key words	Scaled response questions Staff focus groups	What support can be put in place for staff who remain less confident?
Resource check	Submitting resources	What support or time can be given if resources need further work?
Delivery in lessons	Lesson observations	Time taken to carry out learning walks and who conducts them? How is feedback given to staff?

Staff training

Schools are all unique. Even within Multi Academy Trusts where aspects of provision can be standardised, you will never have two schools or settings with identical characteristics. This is a wonderful thing, but of course means that no schools have identical starting points.

What preparedness is there within the individual settings around vocabulary? Schools may already have existing approaches to teaching vocabulary and while there is likely to be similarities between schools on this as broad principles often play out in this area, it does not mean they are identikit models.

Equally, one school in a group may have no pre-existing vocabulary approach. So what might all this mean in terms of initial launch and training sessions around a new approach? Does the vocabulary transition approach chosen demand rigid adherence from all schools that will enable a consistent delivery, or is there a broad framework within which elements of flexibility are permitted to reflect differences between the schools?

Box 8.3 School vocabulary audit template

All responses can be provided on a scale of 1 (strongly disagree) to 5 (strongly agree)

1. Staff are aware of curriculum content for the preceding/succeeding phase in their subject area(s).
2. Curriculum planning takes into consideration the challenge of the transition.
3. There is a coherent existing vocabulary strategy.
4. The value of vocabulary is understood by all staff.
5. Vocabulary strategies are delivered by all staff.
6. Vocabulary is featured in relevant curriculum planning.
7. Vocabulary resources are well developed in all years or subject areas.
8. Pupil vocabulary knowledge is checked in a coherent way.
9. Gaps in pupil vocabulary knowledge are responded to.
10. There are members of current staff who could successfully deliver training on vocabulary to the wider staff.

What do the different starting points for schools and staff mean in terms of training? Can and should training take place among all staff at the same time? Or does one school or sub-group of schools require an earlier start date to lay certain foundations?

The batch of questions above will need to be asked by the leadership group and some may be easy enough to answer immediately. Others may require further exploration and data gathering, whether that be in the form of audits or staff questionnaires. If looking to deploy such tools it will be important to consider the workload for those creating and collating the results, and for the staff being expected to complete them. The time taken to gather the information will also need to be factored into timelines for the project and its launch.

The 5Ws of word selection

We have looked at the nature of some of the decisions that face practitioners when selecting the words, but here we want to think about the wider logistics of how that plays out among groups of feeder primaries and a secondary school.

The interesting interaction between the KS2 and KS3 lists in Chapter 7 provides a fascinating opportunity to discuss selection between the phases. The Education Endowment Foundation's School Transition Tool[3] identifies curriculum continuity as essential to supporting a successful transition so considering the logistics of how phase or transition leaders may work together to select appropriate words is likely to be time well spent. The 5 Ws can help scaffold this time.

Who does the selection?

Earlier in this chapter we spoke about establishing a strategic leadership group. They could also be responsible for aspects of selection, but equally it would be of no surprise if responsibility passed here to other colleagues with greater expertise in relevant curriculum areas.

When does the selection happen?

As the section on selection emphasised, the time required to choose words should not be underestimated. When putting together a timeline requisite space needs to be found for this process. This may require a meeting(s) of key people or time protected for key staff from primary and secondary schools to undertake the selection.

Why pick certain words?

We would reiterate at this juncture the option for the list of words from the project to be used as a starting point to interact with curriculum expertise from primary and secondary phases to enable choices to be made. See Chapter 7 for more detail on this stage.

What do pupils already know?

After an initial selection process by staff, it could be well worth a pre-test to ascertain pupil's starting knowledge. This might help trim a couple of words off the list if pupil knowledge of certain words already seems sturdy. As with much formative assessment, results will not necessarily be neat: there might be significant variation in pupil knowledge on certain words. Teachers would need to be alert for what that might mean in terms of future lesson content, and which pupils they check upon with more frequency when reviewing certain words.

Checking pupil understanding may also inform features of the resource development. If answers show up any trends around common misconceptions or gaps in knowledge then resources can be designed to address those issues.

Where do the chosen words go?

Beyond those people who have made the selections, who else needs to know the chosen words? Are they going to be displayed in classrooms? And leading us on to our next section, what resources need to be created with these words?

Constant evolution

Box 8.4   Case study: Stanley Road Primary, Oldham

As with many schools, we started with discrete word of the day type activities and while there are perhaps speed benefits to this in terms of getting an approach to vocabulary up and running, we felt it was probably lacking in terms of long-term retention.

It was around this time that we were beginning a curriculum rewrite which provided a good opportunity to embed vocabulary in a more strategic way. As we began to specify the detail of the knowledge that we wanted pupils to remember, we were able to set out the precise vocabulary that we expected pupils to use and understand.

Each year, we develop each subject's curriculum further, and we are able to make adjustments. This includes the addition or removal of words or adding more emphasis to ones that we were seeing emerge regularly. For example, in History, political was featuring in multiple year groups.

Another key component to our approach is how the vocabulary links to writing tasks within the same lesson so pupils are given the chance to use the words they are learning. In some instances, this has led to a change in the type of writing being produced so the language can be used more authentically. For example, a unit of work on the Vikings that includes the concept of invasion now includes an expository essay task instead of asking pupils to write a story where they might imagine they are Vikings sailing over to England.

Andrew Percival, Deputy Headteacher – Curriculum, Teaching and Learning; Research Lead

Resources

What does the approach look like? Can you show me?

Of course, I might need to go into a lesson to truly see an approach in action. But failing that, are there resources that have been made that support the approach? Without these a vocabulary approach can be all to easily diluted to some word lists that are occasionally referenced – a hand waved in their direction, as the lessons continue without them at the core. Chapter 7 has further ideas on practical resources that teachers may create to support explicit vocabulary instruction. Beyond their use for practical delivery in the classroom, resource development can also fulfil three other roles:

- Consistency of content between colleagues. This might be deemed crucial to the delivery of the vocabulary approach, but that decision will have been tied into an understanding of the staff vocabulary culture and the needs across different subjects and phases. Will the same method be used across primary and secondary school, or will there need to be flexibility to account for disciplinary literacy requirements?

- A point of return in following years. Having the resources made and saved means the approach already has a better chance of being sustained because there are concrete tools to return to and likely refine in ensuing years.

- Alleviation of workload. This comes with a significant caveat: someone (or perhaps a small sub-group) will need a not insignificant amount of time ring-fenced

Table 8.2 Vocabulary across the transition

Summer term Year 6	Autumn term Year 7
Year 6 teachers deliver content around eight key words	Year 7 teachers check knowledge of the eight key words and re-teach as appropriate

Summer term Year 6	Autumn term Year 7
Year 6 teachers deliver content around five key words	Year 7 teachers check knowledge of the five key words and deliver content around five new ones

to make resources, but if this is done in a coherent manner it can relieve other colleagues of work. Once the resources are made, there will need to be training sessions to share them with teachers who will be using them in the classroom. This creates the space for questions, amendments and ensures there is a shared understanding of how the resources will be used.

The use of the resources in the classroom then requires planning. Who is delivering them and when? Two example models are shown in Table 8.2 to give a sense of different options available.

As an approach becomes more embedded it may be desirable to plan for a really coherent delivery of key concepts that tracks back into Year 5 and continues across a span of three or four years so the transition vocabulary becomes an embedded part of the curriculum. However, any decisions around continuing or extending the work will need to be based on data and evidence around the vocabulary work (see monitoring and evaluation), as well as balancing with other school priorities.

Vocabulary at the transition

Box 8.5 Case study: Huntington Secondary School, Huntington Primary Academy and Yearsley Grove Primary, York

Phase I

Huntington Secondary School undertook a small trial in the summer term of 2022. Two feeder primaries (one control, one intervention) completed questionnaires involving questions around pupil feelings of confidence in terms of the difficulty of work at secondary school, as well as specific questions about key words chosen for English and Geography.

Selection

Eight words were chosen for English and eight for Geography. Eight were chosen to reflect the amount of time available for staff for delivery. Each week, for four weeks, pupils in Year 6 at the intervention school would receive a 30 minute session on two English words and an equivalent session for two Geography words. These sessions were delivered by secondary subject specialists to around 55 pupils in the school hall.

The selection of words was made on two criteria:

a. Using the project corpus as a starting point to look at words more frequently found at KS3

b. Knowledge from secondary staff subject leaders of their curriculum in Year 7 and which words they thought would be most beneficial

Approach to teaching the vocabulary

Sessions would always start with a recap of the words from the previous week before moving on to the new words. The vocabulary sessions were always centred around a Frayer model for the key words. Pupils were always given the definition to ensure consistency. Activities centred around pupils discussing and completing the remaining boxes to unpack the word in more detail.

As part of the pre- and post-questionnaire, pupils were asked multiple choice questions regarding the definition the key words they had been introduced to.

In the intervention group, correct answers in the post-test were on average 20% higher for each word compared to the pre-test. The intervention post-test results were higher than the control school by an average of 18%. While you would expect pupils who had received some direct vocabulary instruction to improve their understanding, the level of improvement in comparison to business as usual meant it was decided to move to phase 2 for the following year.

Phase 2

Among the limitations of phase 1 were:

■ Only one feeder primary received the intervention

■ The delivery model by secondary colleagues was unsustainable if more feeder primaries were to be involved

■ Only two subject areas covered

■ No input from feeder primary around word selection

■ No attempt to see what impact this had on pupil curriculum knowledge or attainment into Year 7

During the Spring of 2023, four feeder primaries were invited to participate in phase 2. The timeline for this phase is described below.

■ Longlist of words (between 10 and 20) selected for all five of the project subject areas. These lists were a combination of the most frequent KS3 words and subject leader additions for words seen as particularly important for the first term of Year 7.

- Primary schools chose from the above their shortlist of words. Their choices were driven by a. knowledge of their curriculum and b. time they created for the delivery of the words.

- Central resources based upon feeder primary word selections were created by Huntington Secondary School. These followed a similar design to phase 1. Feeder primaries were welcome to edit the resources but the objective was to alleviate workload for participating primaries and ensure an element of consistency.

- Year 6 teachers delivered the vocabulary resources to their own classes.

Conclusions around implementation

Carving out time for meaningful conversations and communication about curriculum can feel tricky enough with even your most immediate work colleagues, let alone cross phase involving multiple schools. Knowing the difficulty that will be inherent in creating change in schools we must take great care over our implementation. We have suggested paying heed to the following areas to ensure truly thoughtful planning takes place.

- Strategic leadership

- Monitoring and evaluation

- Staff training

- The 5Ws of word selection

- Resources

While there is never a short cut to effective implementation, the importance of vocabulary to every classroom (or sports hall, or drama studio) at every phase means it can be a genuinely useful rallying point to support pupils. The transition from primary to secondary school is difficult. There will always be challenges for those 11-year-olds making that change. But if we can make some thoughtful and strategic changes to how we support their academic transition, through the framing tool of vocabulary, then we add another support structure in place to enable pupils to succeed at the transition.

Notes

1 Education Endowment Foundation (EEF). 2024. Putting evidence to work: A school's guide to implementation. https://educationendowmentfoundation.org.uk/education-evidence/guidance-reports/implementation

2 Education Endowment Foundation (EEF). 2019. *Putting evidence to work: A school's guide to implementation.*

3 Education Endowment Foundation (EEF). 2021. School transitions tool: A trio of challenges.
    https://educationendowmentfoundation.org.uk/support-for-schools/school-planning-support/3-wider-strategies

9 Conclusion

Marcus Jones and Alice Deignan

This book has described some of what we found as part of the research project 'The linguistic challenges of the transition from primary to secondary school'. The composition of the project team – academics from Leeds and Lancaster Universities, and teachers from primary and secondary schools, with Huntington Research School in York as a hub – was important to its success. The collaboration brought strengths from both sides: academic theory and hands-on expertise in working with young people. Everyone on the team learned from these multiple perspectives and got new insights into their own work.

We hope that the sections and chapters on topics like register, collocation and polysemy were interesting and thought-provoking. We think that there are trends and ideas arising from the data collected by the project that can be useful for schools. However, we were always conscious of the fact that research in isolation can often seem full of interesting ideas, but nonetheless still distanced from the reality of classrooms. We were equally cognisant of the fact that explicit projects looking at a vocabulary approach at the transition were not widespread.

We have tried to give some practical, workable ideas for school-based colleagues to develop this area. Broad, but sound principles around vocabulary instruction, combined with thoughtful implementation, will, we hope, give schools the opportunity to start adding to their existing work around the transition.

In Chapter 7, we have offered 'Depth, connectivity and longevity' as tools for vocabulary selection. And for effective instruction of the chosen words, 'Define, know, record and check' are potentially handy stages to ensure pupils move beyond just a definition.

In Chapter 8, we acknowledged the difficulty of making changes at school, including competing demands for staff time – transition is unlikely to be the only thing on a school's to-do list. Added to this, is the fact that by its very definition, the transition from primary to secondary will involve more than one school, multiplying the possible barriers and hurdles to strong implementation. However, with careful strategic leadership, including perhaps the chance to build the approach to

DOI: 10.4324/9781032645513-10

vocabulary at the transition in stages, we believe that schools can make meaningful steps that support pupils to make this academic step.

What we have had re-confirmed by our work with the thirteen schools that contributed to the project is that there remains a hugely committed body of staff in education who strive to support pupils in ever better ways. We met people who, despite their huge workload, were willing to give up time to talk to us and who were open to any possibilities that could help children further. Similarly, the pupils we spoke to in the focus group interviews, from a cross-section of abilities, seemed, to us, mostly thoughtful and engaged learners. On the whole, pupils look positively, though with understandable trepidation, at the move from primary to secondary. They want to learn and do well. We hope that some of the findings of the project can go some way to augmenting even further the astonishing level of support schools already offer to pupils at the transition. If we have succeeded in contributing a little in this way, we will feel very thankful.

APPENDIX I
The general academic vocabulary of KS3

The following word families are statistically more frequent in our KS3 corpus than in our KS2 corpus. They all appear in at least two of the five subject areas we studied (English, Maths, Science, History, and Geography), mostly three or more.

Words marked with * have different meanings in some different subjects or with everyday language. See Appendix 2 for corpus examples of these.

Absorb

Accurate

Act*

Alternate*

Analyse

Analysis

Annotate

Apply*

Area*

Atmosphere*

Attitude

Average

Barrier*

Charge*

Compound*

Concentration*

Connection

Conservation*

Conserve*

Constant

Construct

Continuous

Control*

Corresponding*

Crucial

Data

Decrease

Density

Detect

Device*

Distance*

Effect*

Element*

Energy*

Engage

Environmental

Equipment

Evaluate

Evaluation

Expand*

Expansion*

Explore

Express*

Expression*

Exterior*

Factor*

Force*

Frequency

Function*

Graph

Hypothesis

Identify

Increase

Independent*

Indicator

Interior*

Interpretation

Investigation

Isolate*

Judgement

Lack

Law

Mass*

Message*

Mode

Negative

Nerve*

Object

Observation

Originally

Outline

Parallel*

Particle

Pattern*

Plot*

Positive

Power*

Potential

Practical

Precise

Pressure*

Property*

Proportion

Random*

React*

Reaction*

Reduction

Reflection*

Relationship*

Release*

Respond

Result*

Review

Sample*

Scale

Scenario

Sector

Series

Separation

Significant*

Simplify

Site

Solution*

Speed

State*

Store*

Strength

Structure

Substance

Substitute

Summary

Surroundings

System

Technique

Tension*

Transfer

Transformation

Treatment*

Typical

Variable

Variation

Wave*

Weight*

APPENDIX 2
Polysemous words

The following words had different meanings in different subjects, and/ or a different meaning in everyday English. We have not separated parts of speech (noun, verb, etc.). We have given corpus examples for the meanings we found, but this can never cover everything! We used the 'BNC' = British National Corpus, a corpus of non-specialist British English, to represent everyday, non-school language. We also used the BNC2014 Spoken, a spoken corpus, to supplement this.

act

The forces *acting* on this rocket-powered car are unbalanced. Year 7 Science textbook.

Many working class men had campaigned for the vote and felt betrayed at the terms of the 1832 Reform *Act.* Year 8 History presentation.

In a crowd people can *act* better than they normally would. BNC

alternate

Lines AB and MN cannot be parallel because *alternate* angles must be equal. Year 8 Maths presentation.

The cone therefore vibrates in time with the *alternating* current through the coil. Year 8 Science worksheet.

He was seen lunching with them on *alternate* days. BNC

apply

We need to *apply* a force in order to change speed. Year 7 Science presentation.

It was two and we're *applying* a scale factor of three. Year 7 Maths teacher talk.

It's specifically written for the job you're *applying* for in mind. Year 7 English teacher talk.

Anyone who needs the service can *apply*. BNC.

area

okay so the *area* of the shaded regions highlighted in green would be the *area* of the rectangle minus the *area* of the semicircle. Year 8 Maths teacher talk.

The *area* was neglected and run down, not the tourist *area* we think of today. BNC.

atmosphere

Oxygen is released back into the *atmosphere*. Year 8 Science textbook.

How does this help to create a ghostly *atmosphere*? Year 8 English presentation.

Sunsets are reddened by dust in the *atmosphere*. BNC.

... a sense of humour lightens the *atmosphere*. BNC.

barrier

It acts as a *barrier* which stops infections and harmful substances from reaching the foetus. Year 7 Science textbook.

... to encourage the East German government to build a *barrier* in Berlin to divide the East and West sectors of the city. Year 8 History textbook.

Age is no *barrier* for Gordon. BNC.

charge

The current is the amount of *charge* flowing per second. Year 8 Science textbook.

How much would she have paid if the service *charge* had not been added? Year 8 Maths worksheet.

Lady Macbeth is still trying to be in *charge*. Year 7 English teacher talk.

...awaiting trial on a *charge* of conspiracy to murder. BNC.

... extra *charges* the guest incurs.. BNC

compound

Can anybody name me the elements found in that *compound*? Year 7 Science teacher talk.

Can you identify a simple sentence and a *compound* sentence? Year 7 English teacher talk.

£4000 earns *compound* interest of 1% a year. How much is it? Y7 Maths worksheet.

concentration

6 million people, mainly Jews, had been killed in *concentration* camps. Year 7 English presentation.

Explain the difference between the strength of an acid and the *concentration* of an acid. Year 7 Science assessment.

There is a large *concentration* of insects here. Year 8 Geography worksheet.

It teaches you qualities such as self-discipline, *concentration* and motivation. BNC.

conservation

The World Wildlife Fund is a *conservation* group that helps to protect Arctic environments. Year 8 Geography presentation.

Does this fit with the law of *conservation* of mass? Year 7 Science presentation.

conserve

Mass is *conserved* in chemical reactions and in physical changes. Year 7 Science textbook.

The treaty bans the disposal of nuclear waste, therefore *conserving* the environment. Year 8 Geography presentation.

control

List all the variables that you would need to *control*. Year 7 Science textbook.

How did missionaries and explorers help expand British *control*? Year 8 History worksheet.

corresponding

Good, *corresponding* angles only work with parallel lines. Year 8 Maths teacher talk.

You are about to see four pictures and a *corresponding* letter. Year 8 History presentation.

… a *corresponding* reduction in the amount of land. BNC

device

Electrical *devices* are slightly different because not all of them are powered by a battery. Year 8 Science teacher talk.

Can you find these presentational *devices* in the brochures? Year 7 English presentations.

Just anything that's a Samsung *device* will use the same connector. BNC2014 Spoken.

They've just left you to your own *devices*. BNC2014 Spoken.

distance

… a wavelength which is the *distance* from one point on a wave to the same point on the next wave.. Year 7 Science textbook.

Macbeth stares thoughtfully into the *distance*. Year 7 English presentation.

We finally saw some light in the *distance*. BNC2014 Spoken.

effect

Some medicinal drugs also have unwanted side *effects*. Year 8 Science textbook.

Explore the *effect* that the writer is trying to create. Year 7 English presentation.

element

Still using your periodic table name an *element* in group two. Year 7 Science teacher talk.

Poe's works were generally macabre in their nature and often had an *element* of mystery about them. Year 8 English reading extract.

we live in a capitalist system.. but there's *elements* of it that are more what you'd call socialist. Year 8 History teacher talk.

energy

… decrease of the battery's chemical *energy* equals the increase of the surroundings' thermal *energy*. Year 8 Science teacher talk.

… the *energy* and enthusiasm of everybody getting involved. BNC

expand

Expand each bracket first then simplify these expressions. Year 8 Maths worksheet.

When heated the metals *expand* by different amounts. Year 8 Science assessment.

Napoleon decided to invade Portugal and *expand* the French empire. Year 7 History reading extract.

expansion

The aim behind this was to buy time for the Soviet Union in the face of Nazi *expansion*. Year 8 History textbook

… using our multiplication and *expansion* skills. Year 7 Maths presentation.

express

What feelings does he *express* towards Catherine and the Lintons? Year 8 English assessment.

Probability can be *expressed* as a fraction, a decimal or a percentage. Year 8 Maths presentation.

I couldn't even *express* myself properly. BNC2014 Spoken.

expression

Substitute numerical values into *expressions*. Year 7 Maths assessment.

Babies communicate with body movements and facial *expressions*. BNC.

exterior

> Pairs of interior and *exterior* angles add up to 180 degrees. Year 7 Maths presentation.

> He had a definite air of strain under the confident *exterior*. BNC

factor

> A *factor* divides exactly into the number. Year 7 Maths presentation.

> Describe some *factors* that may lead to extinction. Year 8 Science textbook.

> What *factors* do you think could have caused the British Empire to fall? Year 8 History presentation.

force (noun only)

> Which *force* means the parachute slows you down? Year 7 Science presentation.

> The British used their armed *forces* to set up colonies. Year 8 History textbook.

> The story ends with the narrator seeming to believe that some supernatural *force* had indeed been at play. Year 8 English reading extract.

> … the armed *forces*… the driving *force*… the labour *force* …police *force*. BNC

function

> The components of a cell each have different *functions*. Year 7 Science textbook.

> Complete the table and draw the graph for each *function*. Year 8 Maths worksheet.

> Draw a line to match each sentence to its correct *function*. Year 7 English assessment.

> You're better off going to this hotel cos they've got a better *function* room. BNC2014 Spoken.

independent

> Identify the *independent* variable. Year 7 Science presentation.

> By the middle of 1776, many Americans had come to the conclusion that they should be fully *independent* from Britain. Year 8 History teacher.

> … an *independent* and intelligent Victorian woman, [she] was born in 1850. English Year 8 teacher talk.

> She's clearly not very *independent* is she? BNC2014 Spoken.

interior

> The angles inside the shape at each corner are called the *interior* angles. Year 8 Maths presentation.

> She has her own *interior* design business. BNC.

isolate

> ... how to make and *isolate* pure salt. Year 7 Science presentation.

> Lenin's Russia became dangerously *isolated*. Year 8 History textbook.

> She suddenly felt terribly alone and *isolated* in this remote corner of England. BNC.

mass

> No atoms are lost or made during a chemical reaction so the *mass* of the products equals the *mass* of the reactants. Year 7 Science presentation.

> The *mass* of a rock is reduced by 22%. Year 8 Maths worksheet.

> There's two different air *masses* meeting and that's led to frontal rainfall. Year 7 Geography teacher talk.

> It was certainly one of the first *mass* political movements in Britain's history. Year 8 History reading extract.

> There was a shout of joy from the *mass* of people on the shore. Year 8 English assessment.

message

> What do you think is the poet's *message*? Year 7 English teacher talk.

> Cannabis tricks brain cells into sending abnormal *messages*. Year 7 Science presentation.

> She left a *message* this morning saying call me back. BNC2014 Spoken.

mode

> The *mode* is the most common piece of data. Year 7 Maths presentation.

> It doesn't matter if it goes into standby *mode* cos I'm not on that. BNC2014 Spoken.

nerve

> ... vibration transferred to the cochlea, whose special hairs trigger the *nerve* signal sent to the brain. Year 8 Science worksheet.

> I have to turn the fan off in the office because it just gets on my *nerves*. BNC2014 Spoken.

parallel

> This is a *parallel* circuit because there is more than one loop. Year 8 Science textbook.

> These are called co-interior because they're sat inside two *parallel* lines. Year 8 Maths teacher talk.

> The novel deals with *parallels* and contrasts. Year 8 English assessment.

pattern

Group 1 elements show *patterns* in physical and chemical properties. Year 8 Science textbook.

Follow the *pattern* to write down the next three terms and describe the rule that you used. Year 7 Maths worksheet.

You start to explore different sound *patterns* don't you. Year 7 English teacher talk.

Plain walls with a border *pattern*. BNC

plot

Having filled in your table you *plot* your graphs then you draw a line through all of the points ... Year 8 Maths teacher talk.

... *plots* of land. Year 8 Geography presentation.

Can you please write your final sentence making sure you've got your *plot* line secure. Year 7 English teacher talk.

power

It's D to the *power* of nine for that one. Year 7 Maths teacher talk.

We've got coal, oil and gas *power* stations. Year 8 Science teacher talk.

The storm left more than 100,000 homes without *power* in Southern Florida. Year 7 Geography reading extract.

Think about the methods that have been used to take *power*. Year 8 History presentation.

pressure

The deeper the water the greater the *pressure*. Year 8 Science presentation.

Peer *pressure* is a key factor in understanding the problem. BNC.

property

Explain the *properties* of solids in terms of the arrangement of particles. Year 7 Science presentation.

... the reluctance of landowners to permit access to their *property*. BNC.

random

This is not *random* as clearly the number 2 has a far higher chance of coming up. Year 8 Maths worksheet.

Just stick on the radio and it comes out with *random* music and you'll either like it or you don't. BNC2014 Spoken.

react

Some metals, for example magnesium/ copper, do not *react* with dilute hydrochloric acid. Year 7 Science presentation.

How the government *reacted* to the protests of the people. Year 8 History presentation.

What words make you *react* in a strong way? Year 7 English presentation.

reaction

Since 1930 some new elements have been made by nuclear *reactions*. Year 8 Science worksheet.

Describe Lockwood's *reaction* to the child he hears and explain why he acts in the way he does. Year 8 English assessment.

reflection

The *reflection* appears the same distance away on the other side of the mirror. Year 7 Maths presentation.

... a sad *reflection* on human nature. BNC.

relationship

There is a multiplier *relationship* between the two variables. Year 8 Maths teacher talk.

The *relationship* between greenhouse gases and other factors is still under study. Year 8 Science reading extract.

He decides to secretly send murderers to kill Banquo meanwhile his *relationship* with his wife is changing. Year 7 English teacher talk.

release

Both reactions *release* energy and produce carbon dioxide. Year 8 Science teacher talk.

He just *released* a new album with his like rock metal band. BNC2014 Spoke.

result

You should have finished your diagram, got your *results* table... Year 8 Science teacher talk.

Those countries that suffered as a *result* of being ruled by another country... Year 8 History textbook.

They're saying now that universities shouldn't focus so much on students' examination *results*. BNC2014 Spoken.

sample

You're gonna test it again take another *sample*. Year 8 Science teacher talk.

Write a *sample* paragraph that aims to use every sentence type. Year 8 English worksheet.

scatter

> Draw a line of best fit where possible for each of the following *scatter* diagrams. Year 7 Maths teacher talk.

> Letters and papers were *scattered* everywhere. BNC.

significant

> What is the difference between rounding to *significant* figures and rounding to decimal places? Year 8 Maths presentation.

> ... the distances involved in travelling make inaccessibility a *significant* challenge for people in Alaska. Year 8 Geography presentation.

> There were also *significant* acts of resistance within Africa itself. Year 8 History reading extract.

solution

> I'll draw it here so try and copy down my *solutions*. Year 7 Maths teacher talk.

> You're going to put some of this starch *solution* into a boiling tube like this. Year 8 Science teacher talk.

> The story is a true mystery. It can have no *solution* as it is about the impossibility of ever knowing what is real. Year 8 English reading extract.

state

> The communists had been defeated and the newly independent state of Malaysia was created as a non-communist *state*. Year 8 History textbook.

> Compare and contrast chemical reactions with changes of *state*. Year 7 Science presentation.

store

> ... a battery is a *store* of energy. Year 7 Science presentation.

> This job involved making wooden barrels used for *storing* and preserving things. Year 7 History presentation.

> The recession is hitting the *stores* hard. BNC.

substitute

> *Substitute* the values of a and b into the second expression. Year 7 Maths presentation.

> Cottage cheese can be *substituted* for full fat cheese. BNC.

tension

> Can you chart the rise of *tension* between these chapters? Year 7 English teacher talk.

Increasingly *tension* grew between the Soviets and the USA and their allies. Year 8 History textbook.

Objects which are stretched or under *tension*... Year 8 Science presentation.

treatment

Check the emergency *treatment* given. Year 7 Science worksheet.

.. to write with imaginative *treatment* of appropriate materials.. Year 8 English assessment.

wave

This diagram shows the amplitude and wavelength of a *wave*. Year 7 Science textbook.

Aren't the winds just blowing the *waves* onto the shore and off the shore? Year 8 Geography teacher talk.

weight

We've got the *weight* acting downwards and we've got what we call the reaction force acting upwards. Year 7 Science teacher talk.

There's little doubt about what the *weight* of opinion was there. BNC.

Index

Note: Page numbers in **bold** indicate boxes or tables.

Printed in the United States
by Baker & Taylor Publisher Services